ENGLISH FOR WORK

EVERYDAY BUSINES
WRITING

Ian Badger & Sue Pedley

Longman

Pearson Education Limited
Edinburgh Gate, Harlow,
Essex, CM20 2JE, England
and Associated Companies throughout the world

www.longman.com

First published 2003
ISBN 0 582 53972 2

Set in Univers Condensed 10pt
Printed in Great Britain by Scotprint, Haddington

Designed and typeset by Rock Graphics

Illustrations by Roger Fereday

Acknowledgements
We would like to thank Helen Parker for her help in developing this series, Maggie Jo St
John, Christine Johnson, Julie Nowell, Teresa Miller and Maria Keller for their valuable
input and Diane Winkleby for her help with the British/American differences boxes.
We would also like to thank Hans-Juergen Prell at Deutsche Telekom and learners from
UPM-Kymmene Oy, Metso Paper Valkeakoski Oy, Metso Paper AB Sundsvall, Hagfors and
Grästorp, Goldwell Gmbh, Business and Medical English Services and Filton College,
Bristol for piloting and reporting on the materials.

Cover photograph copyright © Photonica

Contents

Introduction

English for Work

The books in this series present and practise spoken English and practical writing for everyday communication; they feature key words and expressions which will help you in a wide range of work situations. The target language is introduced through short texts, and developed in language notes and practice exercises.

At the back of each book there is a glossary which contains highlighted language from the texts. Translations of the glossary, in selected languages, can be downloaded from the Longman website, **www.longman-elt.com**.

The series is intended for intermediate level learners. *Everyday Business Writing* will be useful supplementary material if you are preparing for business English examinations such as the University of Cambridge Business English Certificate (BEC), particularly the Reading and Writing paper, and the London Chamber of Commerce and Industry (LCCI) English for Business exam.

Everyday Business Writing

Everyday Business Writing is suitable for anyone who uses English in the business world, and for students learning vocational English in adult education classes, schools, colleges and universities.

The book focuses on everyday business writing, which, in today's business world, is usually sent by email. The book also contains some examples of other types of writing such as letters, memos, telephone messages and cover notes.

Emails are often short and can be very informal. However, even if an email is informal, it should still be accurate, appropriate and easy for the reader to understand. Emails can also be formal – for example when writing to someone for the first time, your email can be just as formal as a letter. There is no standard style for email writing and the book reflects this fact in the range of language presented. One point to note here is the use of contractions. Some people tend to use contractions (I'll call you); others write using full forms (I will call you). In more formal letter writing, full forms are recommended; in emails either form is used.

You may find the other titles in this series helpful:

Everyday Business English
Everyday Technical English
Business Presentations

How to use the book

First of all, work through Unit 1 – The basics. This unit sets out basic guidelines for writing emails and provides examples of style and layout. You can then either work through the book unit by unit or choose one that meets your immediate need. Note that in most of the examples, the focus is on the body of the email. The *Subject box* and *To/From* boxes for example are not always included.

You can use the contents page to search for different types of written documents. Start each chapter by looking at the Useful phrases. Then read the texts and study the accompanying notes. Certain phrases have been highlighted that have particular features associated with them. However, it is worthwhile noting other phrases that appear in the texts, which are equally important and can also be seen as key phrases. Use a dictionary to check your understanding of the language presented and refer to the appendices at the back of the book.

On the notes pages you will find information on some differences between everyday British and American usage.

After studying the texts and notes, work through the exercises; refer back to the texts and notes as necessary. You will find answers to the exercises at the end of the book.

Finally, refer to the glossary at the back of the book and test yourself on your understanding of the highlighted key expressions. Write translations of these expressions, again using a dictionary if necessary. Visit the *English for Work* pages on the Longman website where you will find translations of the Glossary in a selected number of languages.

You can use this book for self-study or with a teacher. Good luck and enjoy building your 'Everyday Business Writing' skills!

Ian Badger and Sue Pedley, Bristol 2003

Some recommended materials to accompany the *English for Work* series:

Longman Business English Dictionary
Penguin Quick Guides: Business English Phrases
Penguin Quick Guides: Business English Verbs
Penguin Quick Guides: Business English Words

1 The basics

Some useful phrases.

How are you?
How did the meeting go?
It went very well.
It was good to talk to you yesterday.
I enjoyed meeting you last week.

Thank you for your message.
I've attached a copy of my report.
Everything looks fine.
No changes needed.
Laurent – please make the arrangements.

Please call me.
Please do not hesitate to contact me.
I look forward to meeting you on Friday.
Look forward to hearing from you soon.
See you next week.
All the best.

Beginnings and endings

The writers know each other well

Subject:	Leadership course

Hi Kim
How are you? It was good to talk yesterday.
I'm finalising the details of the Leadership Course and I want to be sure that everything is correct. Can you check the brochure again before it goes to the printer, especially pages 5 – 7? Please email me or call me on my mobile if any changes are needed.
Best regards
Anders

Subject:	Re: Leadership course

Anders
Everything looks fine. **No changes needed.** See you next week.
All the best
Kim

The writers know each other

Subject:	Meeting 25 May

Dear Ms Novotna
It was good to meet you at the conference last week. I would like to invite you to visit us on Monday 25 May at 11:15 so that we can continue our discussions. I hope that you can come.
Yours sincerely
Piki Gonzales (Mrs)
Head of Personnel

Subject:	Re: Meeting 25 May

Dear Mrs Gonzales
Thank you for the invitation. **I look forward to meeting you** again on 25 May at 11:15 a.m.
Yours sincerely
Tarja Novotna

The writers do not know each other

Subject:	Insurance policy number RT4968

Dear Sir/Madam
I would like to check our insurance cover. We will be shipping new equipment to our Birmingham office next month. Do we need to change our policy or will it be covered?
Yours faithfully
Dr Slack **(Senior Manager)**

Subject:	Re: Insurance policy number RT4968

Dear Dr Slack
This is to confirm that your current policy covers you and that you do not need to take any further action. If you have any other queries, please do not hesitate to contact me.
Yours sincerely
N. Nuul (Administrator)

Notes

Hi Kim

The way you begin and end a message depends on how well you know the person you are writing to. A good guide is to use the same beginning and ending (or a slightly more formal one) as the other person. In informal emails some people do not use the person's name but start the message: *Hi/Hello/Good morning/afternoon*

How are you?

When you know each other well, you often begin a message with a friendly greeting. Other openings: *Hope you are well. It was good to see you last week.*

I'm finalising the details …

Saying why you are writing:
I'm writing to let you know …
Just a note to let you know …
This is to let you know that …
Note how contracted forms I'm (I am), You're (You are) etc. are informal and often used in emails.

Best regards

The way to end a message is a matter of personal choice, but if you are writing first, it is best to be more formal than too informal. Some other informal endings: *Regards Best wishes All the best Cheers* (very informal UK English)

Anders

You can begin an email by simply writing the person's name at the top of a message.

No changes needed.

Note that the verb *are (No changes <u>are</u> needed)* has been left out here to keep the message short and simple.

Dear Ms Novotna – Yours sincerely

In emails which follow the style of more formal letters, if you open with a name: *Dear Ms/Mrs/Miss/Mr;* you close with *Yours sincerely*. However, in emails the rules are more relaxed – you can begin a message with *Dear* and end it with *Best regards, Best wishes* etc. (see notes above).
Ms is used instead of *Mrs* or *Miss* if you do not know if a woman is married or not. Some women prefer to be called *Ms.*

Piki Gonzales (Mrs)

A little old-fashioned, but when the reader may not know from your name whether you are male or female, you can help by giving your title, e.g. *Piki Gonzales* (Ms) at the end of your message.

I look forward to meeting you …

This is one of the most common phrases used at the end of messages. Note the *–ing* form of the verb which follows *look forward to: I look forward to hearing from you. I look forward to receiving the report.*

Dear Sir/Madam – Yours faithfully

Use *Dear Sir/Madam* in formal messages, if you do not know the person you are writing to. *Dear Sir* is also used. This type of message usually ends with: *Yours faithfully.*

Senior Manager

As this is a first formal email, the writer includes his name and position. In well-established relationships, with frequent communication, this is not necessary.

British/American differences

British	American
Hi Kim	*Hi Kim:*
Note: American style uses a colon (:) after the salutation for business correspondence	
	(Dear Piki:/Dear Sir: or Madam:/To Whom it May Concern:
Yours faithfully	This expression is not used in American English. *Sincerely/Yours truly* would be used instead.
finalising	*finalizing*
mobile (phone)	*cell(ular) phone*
insurance cover (not used in American English)	*insurance policy* (also used in British English)
queries (exists, but not often used in American English)	*questions* (also used in British English)

Basic layout

A standard letter

**Hardy &
Heyward**

7 Nogin Road
Shipsam
Northshire
KT3 49P
UK

18 April 20—

Dear Mr Loelgen,

It was good to meet you at the seminar in Paris. I am going to be in Amsterdam in June and I would like to arrange a meeting with you as you suggested.
We have many new products that I am sure will interest you.
Could you let me know if you are available on June 5th or 6th?
I look forward to hearing from you soon.

Yours sincerely,

Isabel Hardy

Isabel Hardy
Partner

A memo

To: All Heads of Department
From: Pamela Newman
                Director of Corporate Planning
Date: 14 June 20 —
Subject: Agent visit

Please note that Eun Joo, our Korean agent, will be visiting the company next Friday 21 June. You are invited to meet her in the Conference Room at 10:30 a.m.

Eun Joo will give us the latest information on the Korean market, and she will answer any questions you may have. There will be a buffet lunch at midday.

Please confirm that you can attend.

A group email

Subject: Menu
▷ Attachments: *none*

Dear all
I've attached a copy of the menu for the annual dinner. Please let me know what you would like by the end of this week.
Laurent, can you make the arrangements for the music.
Thanks.
Klaus

Notes

Dear Mr Loelgen,

Note that some people prefer to write a comma (,) after *Dear Sir, Yours faithfully,* etc. It is now more usual to leave out the comma in both formal and informal letters and messages.

Be consistent. If you use a comma after *Dear John,* use a comma after *Yours sincerely.*

It was good to meet you at the seminar in Paris.

Remind the reader of the first or previous contact.
Do you remember that we met at the Expo presentation?
We spoke at the recent conference.

... I would like to arrange a meeting with you ...

Open formal correspondence with a clear statement of why you are writing.
I am writing to confirm arrangements.
I would like to check some details with you.

We have many new products ...

The next sentence(s) contain(s) your main message. Other possibilities:
It would be good to continue our discussions.
I would like to show you our new brochure.

Could you let me know if you are available ...

Use *could* to make polite requests:
Could you let me know as soon as possible?
Could you call me?

I look forward to hearing from you soon.

Formal letters usually include a polite final phrase. Other examples:
I look forward to meeting you soon.
Looking forward to your reply.

Please note that ...

Please note that ... is a common way of introducing important information in a formal memo.

Please confirm that you can attend.

Other formal polite requests:
Please reply as soon as possible.
Please contact me by Friday.

Dear all

A common greeting when an email is sent to a group. Other greetings:
Dear everyone
Dear colleagues
Hello everyone (informal)
Note that group emails can also be sent without a greeting.

I've attached a copy of the menu ...

Other ways to indicate that you have attached a file/files to your email.
Here is the menu.
The report is attached.
If you want to be more formal you can say:
Please find attached the report as requested.
Herewith the files you asked for.

Laurent, can you make the arrangements ...

Note how we ask an individual to do something in a message sent to a group.
Use a comma (,) or a dash (–) after the person's name:
John, please call me when you receive this.
Sonia – can you forward this message to Oliver.

British/American differences

Because email is international, the differences in British English and American English styles are becoming fewer (US emails may sometimes be more infomal than UK emails). However, some sectors such as financial, banking and legal prefer formality. In these cases, address people by their titles, avoid contractions and slang, and be concise and to the point.

Practice

1 Match the opening greeting with the most suitable close.

a	Dear Sir	i	Yours faithfully
		ii	All the best
b	Fred	i	Best regards
		ii	Yours sincerely
c	Hi Isabel	i	With very best regards
		ii	See you
d	Dear Dr Somerset	i	Yours sincerely
		ii	Best wishes
e	Hello everyone	i	Yours faithfully
		ii	Regards

2 Tick the phrase in each pair which is more <u>informal</u>.

a i Hi Fausta ☑
  ii Dear Fausta ☐

b i Yours sincerely ☐
  ii Regards ☐

c i No problem. ☐
  ii There is no problem. ☐

d i I would like to invite you to visit our office. ☐
  ii Come and visit our office. ☐

e i Please confirm that you can attend. ☐
  ii Let me know if you can come. ☐

f i Thanks for the dinner. ☐
  ii I would like to thank you for the dinner. ☐

3 Complete the sentences with a preposition.

EXAMPLE: I am very interested . in . coming to the seminar.

a I look forward . . . . hearing from you.

b We met . . . . the Shanghai seminar.

c I'd like to make some changes . . . . the programme.

d Thank you . . . . your message.

e I'll see you . . . . Monday . . . . . 3 p.m.

f Call me . . . . my mobile.

g There will be a buffet lunch . . . . midday.

h I've attached the files you asked . . . .

4 Put the correct form, –ing or infinitive, in these sentences.

EXAMPLE: Please .*Confirm*.. (confirm) that you can come.

a   Can you . . . . (check) the brochure for us?

b   I look forward to . . . . (receive) the document.

c   I enjoyed . . . . (meet) you last week.

d   Mr Lahtinen will be . . . . (visit) Helsinki tomorrow.

e   Could you let me . . . . (know) if everything is OK.

f   How did the meeting . . . . (go) yesterday?

g   I am . . . . (write) to ask you for some advice.

h   This is to . . . . (confirm) our conversation.

5 Match the two parts of the sentences.

1	I'm just finalising	a	the files you asked for.
2	Please let everyone	b	from Head office.
3	I've just had a message	c	come to the meeting.
4	Please confirm that you can	d	meeting you last week.
5	We met recently	e	the arrangements for next week.
6	John	f	know about the arrangements.
7	I really enjoyed	g	please make the necessary arrangements.
8	I have attached	h	in the London office.

6 Order the sentences into a message.

An informal message

a   I couldn't find it this morning.

b   I'll be back in the office

c   Good morning, Ian.

d   Did you send me the map yesterday?

e   Maija

f   The fax number is 9505142.

g   Could you fax it again.

h   later this afternoon.

1   *(c) Good morning, Ian* . . . .

2   . . . .

3   . . . .

4   . . . .

5   . . . .

6   . . . .

7   . . . .

8   . . . .

A formal memo

a	will visit the office on Friday.	e	Marcus Kerimov
b	Dear colleagues	f	by Wednesday at the latest.
c	We would like everyone	g	Please confirm that you are able to attend
d	This is to confirm that Mr Tayama	h	to meet him in Room 21 at 2:30.

1 ....

2 ....

3 ....

4 ....

5 ....

6 ....

7 ....

8 *(e) Marcus Kerimov* ....

7 You are the Human Resources manager in your company. You are organising a one-day conference on 'Health and Safety'. Look at your notes below, and then write a memo to all staff:

- inviting them to the conference
- giving all the details of the conference (subject, date, time etc)
- asking for a reply
- offering to give more information if necessary

Write 40–50 words, using the texts and notes in this chapter to help you.

Memorandum

To ....

From ....

Date ....

Subject ....

Notes

Health and Safety Conference

July 22nd

9 a.m.

Board Room

Buffet lunch – midday

2 Making contact

Some useful phrases.

I have seen the advertisement on your web page.
Could you please send me some more information?

Thank you for your email.
I have attached an application form.
Please return it to us.
Please let me know if you need any further information.

We are writing to inform you that we are organising a meeting in Tokyo.
Can you complete the booking form?
Please take a look at our website.
I look forward to hearing from you soon.

We were very interested to hear about the conference.
We are an established company in the UK.
We export to Brazil.
Looking forward to seeing you in Toronto.

Messages 1

A first contact from an individual

Dear Ms Giles

I have seen the advertisement on your web page and would like to apply for the post of International Marketing Manager. I am currently working as a Marketing Assistant for a publishing company in London.

I would be grateful if you could send me an application form and some information about the post.

Thank you in advance.

Yours sincerely

Jean-Luc Reigniers

An acknowledgement

Dear Jean-Luc

Thank you for your email. I am pleased to attach our online application form and some information about the post, as requested.

Could you also complete the attached questionnaire and return it to us by the end of the week.

I look forward to hearing from you soon.

Best regards

Sara Giles

Human Resources Manager

A reply

Dear Ms Giles

Please find attached my completed application form and a copy of my CV for your information.

I look forward to your reply.

Best regards

Jean-Luc Reigniers

Chasing up information

Dear Jean-Luc

Thank you for your recent application. However, we have not yet received your completed questionnaire. Could you please return this as soon as possible.

Please let me know if you have any queries.

Best regards

Sara Giles

A reply

Dear Ms Giles

Please find attached my completed questionnaire. I apologise for not sending this earlier.

Please call me on my mobile 08120745614 if you need any further information.

Looking forward to hearing from you soon.

Best regards

Jean-Luc Reigniers

Notes

I have seen the advertisement on your web page …

> Emails generally open with a clear point of reference.
> *Thanks for your email.*
> *We met at the conference last week.*
> *I read your report with interest.*

… post …

> *Post* is an alternative word for *job* or *position*.

I am currently working as a Marketing Assistant for a publishing company in London.

> Saying more about your current job:
> *I have been working as a Sales Advisor since May.*
> *I have been in the Export Business for three years.*
> *I have been a lecturer since 2001.*

Thank you for your email.

> This is a standard response to an email.
> When receiving an email from someone for the first time you could also say:
> *Thank you for your interest in our company.*
> *We were pleased to hear that you are interested in …*

I am pleased to attach our online application form …

> Documents sent with an email are *attached* rather than *enclosed* as they are with a letter.
> You could also say:
> *Please find attached …*
> *Please take a look at the attached file …*
> *The attachments will give you the information you need …*

… as requested.

> This is a more common expression than the alternative:
> *… which you requested.*

… CV …

> This is a document giving details of your education and past employment, used when applying for a job. It comes from the Latin: *curriculum vitae.*

I look forward to your reply.

> This phrase is a standard polite close to an email.
> Alternatives are:
> *I look forward to hearing from you soon.*
> *I await your reply.* (very formal)

Please let me know if you have any queries.

> This is a polite, informal ending to the message. You could also say:
> *Please contact us if you have any queries.*
> A more formal ending is:
> *Please do not hesitate to let us know if you require any further information.*
> *Queries* are *questions.* The singular is *query.*

I apologise for not sending this earlier.

> You could also say:
> *I am sorry I did not send this earlier.*
> *I'm sorry I forgot to send it.* (informal)

Please call me on my mobile …

> Note the use of prepositions in the sentences above and below:
> *Please contact me on extension 232.*
> *Please visit our website at www.filton.ac.uk.*
> *You can email me at jlreigniers@emiclidc.com.*

British/American differences

British	American
I have seen the advertisement …	*I saw the advertisement …* Note: American English usually uses the simple past tense.
apologise	*apologize*
CV	*resumé* Note: In American English *CV* is usually reserved for academic applications.
Please call me on my mobile.	*Please call me on my cell phone.*
Please contact me on extension 232.	*Please contact me at extension 232.*

Messages 2

A first contact from a company

Dear Colleague

We are writing to invite you to a conference in Tokyo. This will be an excellent opportunity to meet local suppliers and agents.

Please take a look at our website at www.ic1wz.co.np where you will find details of **the conference schedule** and our online registration form.

Please do not hesitate to contact us if you require any further information.

Yours sincerely

Minori Kishimoto

Conference Organiser

A reply

Dear Ms Kishimoto

We were very interested to hear about **the forthcoming conference** in Tokyo **and would like to attend.** I am pleased to attach our completed registration form and look forward to hearing from you soon.

Yours sincerely

Guillermo Ravallo

A request for further information

Dear Mr Ravallo

We have received your application and are pleased to inform you that we have reserved **a stand** and some video equipment for you, as you requested on your registration form.

Could you please send us a fifty word **summary of your company**, for our conference handbook, **by the end of the week.**

Best regards

Minori Kishimoto
Conference Organiser

Introducing the company

Dear Ms Kishimoto

Thank you for your email. Here is a summary of our company for the handbook:

'**We are an established company in the UK** with over thirty years' experience of providing management training for the **manufacturing and service industries**.

We can provide a range of training programmes, **on-site**, at a **venue** in the UK, or online, at a competitive price.'

I hope this is acceptable. If not please do not hesitate to contact me.

Looking forward to meeting you in Tokyo.

Best regards

Guillermo Ravallo

Notes

We are writing to invite you to a conference ...

In formal written communications it is more common to use the full verb form *We are writing* rather than *We're writing*. Companies will also use *We* rather than *I* when contacting someone for the first time.

Please take a look at our website ...

An alternative is:
Please visit our website ...
You will find our website at ...

... the conference schedule ...

This is a detailed plan of what will happen and when it will happen.
Note that an *itinerary* is the detailed schedule or plan of a visit or trip.

... the forthcoming conference ...

Something which is *forthcoming* will happen soon.

... and (we) would like to attend.

Notice how it is not necessary to repeat *we* in this sentence.

... a stand ...

At a conference or exhibition *a stand* is a small area where a company can display its products or give out information to visitors.

Could you please send us a ... summary of your company ...

A more formal alternative is:
We would be grateful if you could provide us with a summary ...

A *summary* gives the most important facts in a brief way.

... by the end of the week.

By the end of the week is used to say when exactly you want something done. Other alternatives are:
... before Friday.
... on Monday at 9 a.m.
... within the next 24 hours.
... in an hour.

We are an established company in the UK ...

Other ways to describe a company could include:
We are a large manufacturing company specialising in ...
We are one of the leading producers of ...
We are the leading exporters of ...

... manufacturing and service industries.

The *manufacturing industry* makes products to sell to customers, for example cars, telephones, clothes.
The *service industry* provides services and advice to customers. For example banks, travel agents, shops.

... on-site, ...

On-site training is when the trainer goes to the customer's workplace to give the training.

... venue ...

A *venue* is the place where an event (such as a conference or meeting) takes place.

British/American differences	
British	**American**
a stand (for conferences)	*a booth; an exhibit*
experience of ...ing	*experience in ...ing*
organiser	*organizer*
programmes	*programs* (Note: This American spelling of programs is used in British English but only to refer to computer programs.)
venue (not used in this way in American English)	In American English *location* or *site* would be more usual.
specialising	*specializing*

Practice

1 Complete the sentences with a preposition.

EXAMPLE: We are a leading exporter .of. electrical goods.

a   I am currently working . . . . a Financial Advisor.

b   I would like to apply . . . . the position of Chief Executive.

c   I have been working . . . . Framco since March.

d   I enclose an application form . . . . requested.

e   I would like the work completed . . . . the end of the week.

f   Please telephone me . . . . 00 39 572 34698.

g   Please email me . . . . sjwood@uh2mx.com for any further information.

h   We are a large manufacturing company specialising . . . . glassware.

2 Match the words with the correct definition.

1	stand	i	Questions you ask to get information or to check something is true or correct.
2	itinerary	ii	The tools or machines you need for a particular activity.
3	equipment	iii	A small area at a conference or exhibition where a company can show its products or give out information to visitors.
4	queries	iv	The place where an event takes place.
5	post	v	A detailed schedule or plan of a visit or trip.
6	venue	vi	A job or a position in a company.

3 Fill in the gaps with words from the box below.

| forthcoming | summary | questionnaire |
| on-site | range | producer | service |

EXAMPLE: We are pleased to invite you to our .forthcoming. conference in Ohio.

a   We can arrange training programmes either . . . . or online.

b   Our company produces a wide . . . . of products.

c   We are the leading . . . . of cars in Germany.

d   The . . . . sector includes businesses such as banks and travel agents.

e   Can you prepare a short . . . . for the monthly report.

f   Could you complete the attached . . . . and return it as soon as possible.

4 Match the two parts of the sentence.

1	If you have any questions	a	to inform you about our next exhibition.
2	I look forward	b	at our website.
3	We are writing	c	for your recent application.
4	We were interested	d	please do not hesitate to contact me.
5	Please take a look	e	to hear about the conference in Madrid.
6	Thank you	f	send me some further information.
7	Could you please	g	to meeting you in September.

5 Put the sentences in the correct order.

1 Please take a look at our website at www.conzfi.co.kr

2 We are writing to inform you

3 Please do not hesitate to contact us

4 where you will find full details of the conference.

5 that we are organising a conference in New York

6 We would like to invite

7 at the end of the month.

8 your organisation to attend.

9 if you require any further information.

Dear Colleague

2 We are writing to inform you ....

....

....

....

....

....

....

....

....

Yours sincerely

Jeongmi Seo

---

6 Match the statement in A with the response in B.

A

1 I attach our completed registration form for the forthcoming exhibition.

2 I would like to apply for the post of Finance Officer.

3 We have not yet received your completed application form.

4 We would like to invite you to our conference in London.

B

a We were interested to hear about the conference, and would like to attend.

b Thank you for your application. We have reserved a stand for you in the main hall.

c Thank you for your email. I am pleased to attach our online application form.

d I apologise for not sending this earlier.

7 Read the email and notice below and then complete the booking form. Write a word or phrase or a number on lines 1 – 5.

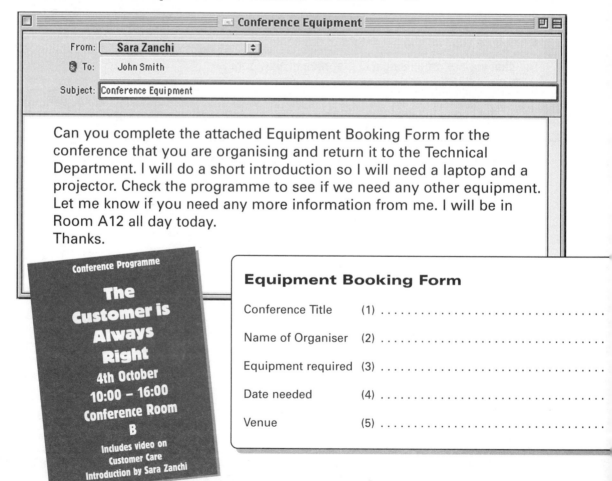

Conference Equipment

From: Sara Zanchi

To: John Smith

Subject: Conference Equipment

Can you complete the attached Equipment Booking Form for the conference that you are organising and return it to the Technical Department. I will do a short introduction so I will need a laptop and a projector. Check the programme to see if we need any other equipment. Let me know if you need any more information from me. I will be in Room A12 all day today.
Thanks.

Conference Programme

The Customer is Always Right

4th October
10:00 – 16:00
Conference Room B

Includes video on Customer Care
Introduction by Sara Zanchi

Equipment Booking Form

Conference Title (1) ....

Name of Organiser (2) ....

Equipment required (3) ....

Date needed (4) ....

Venue (5) ....

3 Arrangements

Some useful phrases.

We would be very pleased if you could visit our company.
Please let us know your availability.
Are you free on Monday afternoon?

Can you send me a map please?
I've attached a map and directions to our office.
See you Friday.
I look forward to seeing you tomorrow.

I've put together an itinerary for the China trip.
I'm taking the 7:30 flight to Paris tomorrow morning.
I'm writing to confirm my hotel reservation.

I'm sorry I wasn't free.
I've been delayed in Paris.
He's missed his flight.
I'll be away from my office for a few days.

I tried to ring you back yesterday.
The number was engaged.
I'll call again tomorrow.

Arranging a visit

An invitation

Dear Ms Dunn

We were interested to hear that you will be in Japan for the International Motor Conference, and **we would be very pleased if you could visit our company** during your stay in Tokyo.

Please let us know your availability and we will arrange a tour of our factory.

We hope to have the opportunity of meeting you soon.

Yours sincerely
Mr Taro Sato

Replying to an invitation

Dear Mr Sato

Thank you for the invitation to visit your company. I would be very interested in seeing your factory, as I have heard excellent reports on your latest production line technology.

I will be available on 6th May if this is convenient for you.

I look forward to your confirmation.

Yours sincerely

Ms Gloria Dunn

A confirmation

Hi John

Just to confirm your visit to us on Friday May 31 at 10 a.m.

If you come to reception and ask for me, I will meet you there.

If you need to contact me, please call me on my mobile (07975 639400).

See you Friday.

Regards
Kevin

Sending directions

Dear Miss Bromley

I am pleased you are able to visit us on 21st. **I am attaching a map** with directions to our **facility**, in case you need it. Please let me know when you hope to arrive.

When you arrive at the main gate, Security will give you a visitor's pass. **Follow the road around to the main reception**, where I have reserved a car park space for you.

Looking forward to meeting you next week.

Regards

Jacob Letterman

Chasing up information

Dear Miss Bromley
I'm just finalising arrangements for your visit. **Do you know when you are planning to arrive yet?**
Best regards
Jacob Letterman

Notes

... we would be very pleased if you could visit our company ...

Other similar phrases:
We are holding a conference in London and would be very pleased if you could attend.
We would like to invite you to an evening reception.
This is the formal language of invitation.
More informal ways to invite people would be:
Please join us for lunch tomorrow.
Would you like to visit our new factory?

Please let us know your availability ...

This is a formal way of asking when you are free. You could also say:
When would be convenient?
Are you free on Tuesday?

Thank you for the invitation to visit your company.

This is a formal reply to an invitation from a new contact. Also:
I was very pleased to receive your invitation.
A more informal reply when you know the person well:
Thanks for inviting me.
Thanks for the invite.

I look forward to your confirmation.

You can also say:
Could you please confirm this?
Can you confirm as soon as possible?

Just to confirm your visit to us ...

This is an informal way of confirming details. A more formal way of saying this would be:
I am writing to confirm details of your visit to our company next week.

See you Friday.

This is an informal ending to an email confirming a planned meeting/visit. A more formal ending would be:
I look forward to meeting you on Friday.

I am attaching a map ...

Detailed directions are often sent as attachments. If directions are very short, you could say:
Leave the motorway at Junction 14, turn left on to the A37. Our office is one mile along this road on the left.

facility

This is often used to mean a *factory* or the place where a product is made.

Follow the road around to the main reception ...

Other useful expressions for giving directions:
Follow the main road into town, and you will find us on the right.
Stay on this road until you reach the Hotel.
Keep going straight.
Turn left at the station.
Go straight along the corridor.

Do you know when you are planning to arrive yet?

More informal:
Any news about when you plan to arrive?
More formal:
Please advise your arrival time.

British/American differences

British	American
I tried to ring you back yesterday.	I tried to call you back yesterday. (Also used in British English.)
The number was engaged.	The line was busy.
finalising	finalizing

Some differences in giving directions

British	American
Leave the motorway at Junction 14.	Leave the freeway at exit 14.
One mile along this road.	One mile down this road. (*Down* also used in British English)
Along the corridor.	Down the hall.
Go straight for 100 metres.	Keep going for a block.

Note: metric distances are not used in the US. In towns and cities, distances are expressed in blocks (the distance between two streets).

Travel arrangements

Arranging an itinerary

Helena,

I've put together the following itinerary. Can you let me know what you think about it? **We need to finalise it today.**

Tuesday 22

    Departure from Milan at 11:05 on flight BA68, arriving Manchester at 11:25

    Afternoon visit to Salford site

    Overnight stay at Hilton Hotel, Salford

Wednesday 23

    Pick-up by company car at 08:00

    All day visit to Newcastle on Tyne site

    Return flight to Milan departing at 17:05 on flight BA67, arriving at 19:20

All the best

Michelle

Making a booking

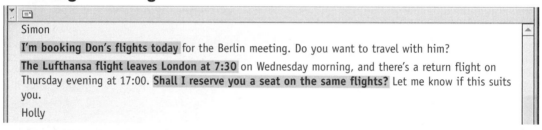

Simon

I'm booking Don's flights today for the Berlin meeting. Do you want to travel with him?

The Lufthansa flight leaves London at 7:30 on Wednesday morning, and there's a return flight on Thursday evening at 17:00. **Shall I reserve you a seat on the same flights?** Let me know if this suits you.

Holly

Confirming a reservation

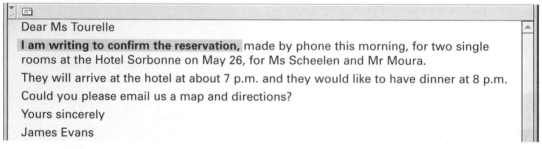

Dear Ms Tourelle

I am writing to confirm the reservation, made by phone this morning, for two single rooms at the Hotel Sorbonne on May 26, for Ms Scheelen and Mr Moura.

They will arrive at the hotel at about 7 p.m. and they would like to have dinner at 8 p.m.

Could you please email us a map and directions?

Yours sincerely

James Evans

Checking travel arrangements

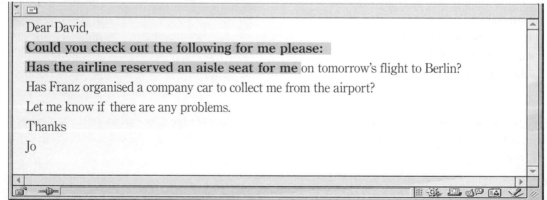

Dear David,

Could you check out the following for me please:

Has the airline reserved an aisle seat for me on tomorrow's flight to Berlin?

Has Franz organised a company car to collect me from the airport?

Let me know if there are any problems.

Thanks

Jo

Notes

I've put together the following itinerary.

An *itinerary* is the detailed timetable of a visit or trip. Other verbs can be used with itinerary:
The agent has changed the itinerary.
I've fixed the itinerary for our Japan trip.

We need to finalise it today.

You can also say:
We'll finalise the details today.
Can we finalise the schedule today?

Departure from Milan at 11:05 on flight BA68, …

Note the following prepositions of place and time when talking about arrangements:
The plane departs <u>from</u> Paris <u>at</u> 8:00.
I'm travelling <u>on</u> Flight KLM646 <u>to</u> Osaka.
We're leaving <u>at</u> midday.
I arrive <u>at</u> Terminal 3 <u>at</u> 19:00.

Pick-up by company car at 8:00

To *pick up* is an informal expression meaning to *collect*.
An airport pick-up can be arranged.
I'll pick you up at the station.

I'm booking Don's flights today …

We often use the present continuous tense to talk about future plans and arrangements:
I'm going to Paris in the morning.
I'm meeting the Finance Director at 2 p.m.
I'm catching the early train.

The Lufthansa flight leaves London at 7:30 …

We often use the present simple tense to talk about timetables:
The train arrives at 18:00.
The conference starts at 9 a.m. tomorrow.
Coaches leave the airport every thirty minutes.

Shall I reserve you a seat on the same flights?

Shall is used in offers, suggestions and requests for advice.
Shall I finish the report for you?
Shall we meet for lunch?
What shall we do about the problem?

I am writing to confirm the reservation, …

Other verbs used with *reservation*:
I'm writing to change my reservation.
I'm afraid I have to cancel my reservation.
Can I check my reservation?

Could you check out the following for me please:

To check out something is an informal way of saying *check*:
Can you check the following for me please:
Can you check out the flight times?
You can also *check out* of a hotel, meaning to pay and leave.
We need to check out before 7:00 to catch our flight.

Has the airline reserved an aisle seat for me …

Other questions you can ask to check arrangements:
Did you reserve a window seat for me?
Have you re-confirmed my flight?
Did you book an economy ticket?

British/American differences

British	American
departing at 17:05	Note: The 24-hour clock is called military time and is not generally used in the US. Times are noted with a.m. and p.m.
a booking/ to book	*a reservation/to reserve* (also used in British English)
travelling	*traveling*
midday	*noon* Note: In American English, *midday* indicates a period of time in the early afternoon, from about noon until 2 p.m.
I've fixed the itinerary.	*I've set/made the itinerary.*
single (ticket)	*one way (ticket)*
In a hotel:	
reception	*front desk*
a single/ double room	Note: hotels in the US use varying terminology but these are usual: *a single* = a room with one double bed *a double* = a room with two double beds *a queen* = a room with one queen size bed *a king* = a room with one king size bed

Taking and forwarding messages

Leaving a message

Li Juan

Thank you for your phone call this morning. **I'm sorry I wasn't free to speak. I tried to call you back this afternoon** to arrange a meeting, but **the number was engaged.** You can call me at the office on 020 7001 1444 – best before 3:30 – or on my mobile 07050 234768.

Sue

Passing on a message

Dear Andreas

*Jayne Baxter called today. **She's been delayed in Shanghai**, so she'll miss the dinner this evening with you and Mr Ho Lim. **Can you give her apologies, please?***

*Can you also tell Mr Ho Lim that **there are still some details to sort out** with the contract? **Can he call her tonight, please** at the hotel?*

Ling Shi

Forwarding a message

Sandy
Hope you had a good break in Italy. **I've just received the draft itinerary for Sweden from Helen. Have a look at it** over the weekend - we can then discuss it on Monday.
Bye for now
Stefan

——Original Message——-
From: Wall, Helen [mailto:Helen.Wall@ie23c.com]
Sent: 29 August 17:37
To: Stefan Ruiz (E-mail)
Subject: Itinerary for Swedish Trip

Dear Stefan
I'm attaching the draft itinerary for Sweden.
Let me know if you want me to arrange any other visits for you.
Helen

An acknowledgment

Thanks for this, Stefan.

It looks fine, but I'll go through it carefully this weekend and we can discuss it on Monday. **Let's say 10 a.m. in my office.**

Sandy

An automatic email reply

I shall be away from the office until 22 July. If you need an urgent reply, please contact Eve Wheeler on 0590 4119456.

Notes

I'm sorry I wasn't free to speak.

Reasons for not being able to talk:
I was on another line.
I was in a meeting.
I was out of the office.
I wasn't free is informal, meaning *I was busy.*
Are you free? means *Are you doing anything?*
Also: *Are you available?*

I tried to call you back this afternoon ...

To call back is to return someone's telephone call.
Can you call back tomorrow?
I'll ask her to call you back.
I tried to return your call.

... the number was engaged.

This phrase means the same as *the number was busy.* Other reasons for not being able to reach someone:
There was no reply.
I had the wrong number.
I couldn't get through.

She's been delayed in Shanghai ...

Some other reasons for not being available:
She's been delayed at the airport.
He's been held up in Paris.
He's missed his flight.

Can you give her apologies, please?

You could also say:
Can you send Sara's apologies?
Please give her apologies.
Can you apologise on her behalf, please?

... there are still some details to sort out ...

To sort out is to solve difficulties or problems.
There's been a misunderstanding; I'll try and sort it out by tomorrow.
We've sorted out the computer system.

Can he call her tonight, please?

Some examples of other messages you can pass on:
Please call Sally today.
Can John fax the report to Franz?
Please let him know David will be late.

I've just received the draft itinerary for Sweden from Helen. Have a look at it ...

You could also say:
Take a look at the itinerary which Helen has sent.
I'm forwarding an itinerary from Helen for you to look at.

Thanks for this, Stefan.

To confirm that you have received something you can send a simple *Thank you.*
You could also say:
Thanks for sending the report.
Many thanks for the sales figures.

Let's say 10 a.m. in my office.

This is an informal way of making an arrangement. You could also say:
What about 10 a.m. in my office?
Can you make 10 a.m?
How about 2 p.m. tomorrow?

I shall be away from the office until 22 July.

Automated email replies are used when you know you will be out of the office for a period of time. Other possibilities:
I will be on leave until 22 August.
I will be away on business until 2 May.
I will be out of the office from Monday 2nd June until Monday 9th June.

British/American differences

British	American
The number was engaged.	*The line was busy.*
There are still some details to sort out.	*There are still some details to take care of.*
the draft itinerary	*a draft of the itinerary*
apologise	*apologize*
I'll try and sort it out by tomorrow.	*I'll try and take care of it tomorrow.*

Practice

1 Complete the sentences A to D below using the words in the box.

~~confirm~~	attend	22nd July	pleased	stay	office
contact	queries	next week	invitation	single	August

a   I'd like to .Confirm.. the reservation for a . . . . room, on . . . .

b   We would be very . . . . if you could visit us . . . .,
during your . . . . in Toronto.

c   Paul is out of the . . . . this week. Please . . . . Maria
on 3650899 if you have any . . . .

d   Thank you for the . . . . to the conference in . . . .
I will be pleased to . . . .

2 Match the two parts of the sentences used in making arrangements.

1	We would be very pleased	a	to your confirmation.
2	I look forward	b	if this is convenient?
3	We would like to invite you	c	on the 9:15 flight to Paris.
4	Could you please let me know	d	for a double room on 26th May?
5	I've reserved a seat for you	e	if you could visit our company.
6	Can you confirm my reservation	f	at the airport at 7 p.m.
7	A company car will pick you up	g	for your China trip.
8	I have organised the itinerary	h	between 8 and 10 a.m.
9	You can call me tomorrow	i	to an evening reception.

3 Put these sentences into the correct order.

a   Our office is located opposite the bus station, next to the Marlin Hotel.

b   Just to confirm your visit to us on Friday 14th at 9 a.m.

c   If you need to contact me for any reason, please call me on my mobile 071186 34527.

d   Looking forward to seeing you on Friday.

e   Best regards, Francis

f   When you arrive, ask for me at reception and I will meet you there.

1   b. Just to confirm your visit to us on Friday 14 at 9 a.m.

2   . . . .

3   . . . .

4   . . . .

5   . . . .

6   . . . .

4 Complete the sentences with a suitable preposition.

EXAMPLE: We will pick you up .by. company car.

a   Go straight . . . . the corridor. Her office is . . . . the left.

b   I'll be . . . . . Madrid next week. I'll stay . . . . . the Moderno.

c   Our driver will meet you . . . . . Terminal 2 . . . . . midnight.

d   There is a flight . . . . . Paris twice a day.

e   I've fixed the itinerary . . . . . the Brazil trip.

f   I'm travelling . . . . . flight BA248 . . . . . Madrid.

5 Check each sentence. Is the preposition in *italics* correct, incorrect or not necessary?

EXAMPLE: They will be arriving ✗ the hotel tonight.   . . . . . . .at. . . . .

a   Eva Gonzales is arriving *from* Madrid tomorrow.   . . . .

b   I did not know that Heidi was visiting *to* Bangkok.   . . . .

c   Erik Sharman is staying *at* the Grand Hotel.   . . . .

d   I will contact *to* Neil for his approval of this budget.   . . . .

e   The itinerary is finalised *from* the Berlin trip.   . . . .

f   Could you please confirm *in* writing?   . . . .

g   He is *off* from his desk at the moment.   . . . .

h   The flight leaves *on* 19:00.   . . . .

6 Read the memo and email below, then complete the Travel Form. Write one word, phrase or number in each numbered space 1 to 5.

M e m o r a n d u m

To: Jaques Duval, Finance
From: Roberta Benetto, Marketing
Date: 21st May
Re: My visit to Beijing - to attend Agents Workshop

Can you look through the flight details from Travel World and complete a Travel Form for me, requesting the flight which arrives early in the morning of the 18th. Could you organise payment today please, by credit card?

Thanks   RB

Roberta
Re your trip to Beijing:
Outward Flights
Two possible flights arriving on 18 June:

Air France	AF 202	Departure London Heathrow	17 June	11:45
		Arrival Beijing	18 June	08:15
British Airways	BA148	Departure London Heathrow	17 June	21:00
		Arrival Beijing	18 June	17:00

Return Flights

Air France	AF 203	Departure Beijing	28 June	10:25
		Arrival London Heathrow	28 June	17:30
British Airways	BA149	Departure Beijing	28 June	13:00
		Arrival London Heathrow	28 June	20:00

Can you confirm within 48 hours please.
Thanks
Sophie
Travel World

Travel Form

Traveller Details

Name   Roberta Benetto

Department   .....1.............................

Purpose of Visit   .....2.............................

Travel Details

Flight from   .....London.........................

Flight to   .....Beijing........................

Departure Date/Time   .....3.............................

Return Date/Time   .....28 June........................

Airline   .....4.............................

Cost   .....€1 000.........................

Method of Payment   .....5.............................

4 Meetings

Some useful phrases.

We need to set up a meeting.
How about next week sometime?
What about Tuesday at 10 a.m. in my office?
Are we still OK for Friday?
We could have a working lunch.

Can you confirm the meeting on the 17th in Prague?
Can you get back to me today?
It's in my diary.
Can we reschedule for Monday?

Can you let me have all agenda items today please?
We'll need to circulate the agenda.
Let me know if you want to make any changes.
We'll need to rearrange the programme.

I've attached the minutes of the meeting.
I was interested to read the action points.
Thank you for your comments.

.

Setting up a meeting 1

Suggesting a meeting

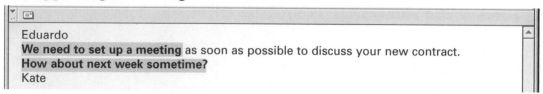

Eduardo
We need to set up a meeting as soon as possible to discuss your new contract.
How about next week sometime?
Kate

Suggesting a date, time and place

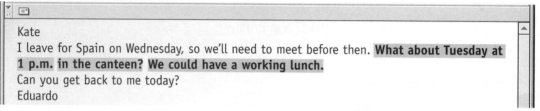

Kate
I leave for Spain on Wednesday, so we'll need to meet before then. **What about Tuesday at 1 p.m.** in the canteen? **We could have a working lunch.**
Can you get back to me today?
Eduardo

Agreeing

Dear Mr Sato
I would be very pleased to visit you next Tuesday, as you suggested. **3 p.m. would be fine with me.** I will be with one of my colleagues, Miss Ashley, our new Production Manager. **I look forward to seeing you again next week.**
Best regards

Ms Sue Winter

Confirming a meeting

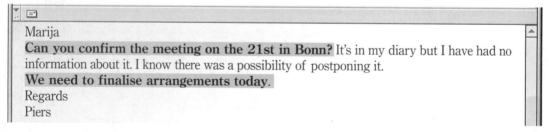

Marija
Can you confirm the meeting on the 21st in Bonn? It's in my diary but I have had no information about it. I know there was a possibility of postponing it.
We need to finalise arrangements today.
Regards
Piers

An urgent meeting

Memorandum

To: all senior managers
From: Rick Lovell, Chief Executive
Date: 20 December

We have a serious problem with the packaging of one of our products.
I want to meet urgently with all senior managers at 2 p.m. this afternoon in my office. **The purpose of the meeting is to brief you on the problem,** decide the action we need to take and discuss how to manage the Media.
Please clear your diaries for the whole of the afternoon.
RL

Notes

We need to set up a meeting …

To set up a meeting is to arrange or organise a meeting. Other useful expressions for setting up a meeting:
I'd like to meet tomorrow.
We are holding a meeting at 2 p.m.
There will be a staff meeting tomorrow.

How about next week sometime?

This is a useful informal expression for suggesting a meeting without giving a specific day or time. You could also say:
How does next week look?
Can you let me know your availability next week? (more formal)

What about Tuesday at 1 p.m. …

This is another informal way of suggesting a meeting. Also:
How about Tuesday at 1 p.m?
More formal suggestions are:
Are you available on Tuesday at 1 p.m?
Can you manage 1 p.m. on Tuesday?
Is 1 p.m. on Tuesday convenient?

… in the canteen?

Other prepositions to describe location:
We'll meet _in_ my office.
The conference is _at_ Cleve House.
We'll meet _on_ platform two _at_ the station.

We could have a working lunch.

A working lunch is when you carry on working while you are eating lunch.

I would be very pleased to visit you next Tuesday, …

This is a formal/polite way of agreeing to a suggested meeting time.

3 p.m. would be fine with me.

Other informal expressions to show acceptance or agreement:
3 p.m. is OK for me.
3 p.m. suits me.
3 p.m. is fine.

I look forward to seeing you again next week.

It is usual to confirm arrangements at the end of the message. More informally you can say:
See you next week.

Can you confirm the meeting on the 21st in Bonn?

This is useful for confirming or checking arrangements. More informal:
Is next Tuesday's meeting in Bonn still on?
Are we still OK for the 21st?

We need to finalise arrangements today.

You can use need to point out the importance of something.
We need to contact him immediately.
You need to check the details carefully.

I want to meet urgently …

To point out the urgency of something use vocabulary such as:
We'll have to do this _immediately_.
This will need _immediate_ action.
This is a _priority_.

The purpose of the meeting is to brief you on the problem, …

To brief someone is to give information about something.

British/American differences	
British	**American**
canteen	café(teria) (also used in British English)
It's in my diary.	It's in my datebook/calendar. Note: In American English a diary (or journal) is a book in which you write down the things that happen to you each day (also in British English).
We'll meet on platform 2 at the station.	We'll meet on/at track 2 at the train station.

Setting up a meeting 2

Setting the agenda

Dear all,

Can you have a look at the agenda for Friday's meeting and let me know as soon as possible if you want to make any changes. **Please let me know in advance if you are unable to attend** for any reason.

Monthly Review Meeting – **Agenda**

Date:	4 August
Time:	10:00
Venue:	Conference Room 2
Participants:	SP IM JK BH RA

1 **Apologies**
2 **Minutes of last meeting**
3 Review of 2nd quarter sales
4 Sales projections for next quarter
5 **AOB**
6 **Date of next meeting**

Thanks

Dan

Changing the agenda

To: Executive Team
From: Don Willis
Date: 21 October
Subject: Agenda item change

Please note the change to item 2 on the agenda for this week's sales meeting. As Sharon Despois will be away, **I have moved the International Strategies paper to next week.**
We now have a slot to discuss Customer Service. Could you all therefore send your reports to Jane by Wednesday? **She will circulate these to everyone prior to the meeting.**

Negotiating changes

Emma

You asked me to present the costs for the CP2 model at tomorrow's meeting. Unfortunately, **our computer system is down** today, so I am not able to access the figures. **Is it possible to put this on the agenda for Monday's meeting?**

Martine

Finalising arrangements

To all departmental managers

Can we meet in my office tomorrow at 8:30 a.m? **I'd like to run through the final arrangements** for the staff induction day on Monday?

We are expecting more than 25 new employees so **we need to ensure that everything runs smoothly.**

Jim Downs

Notes

Please let me know in advance if you are unable to attend ...

> *I am unable to attend* is a formal way of saying *I can't come.*
> *In advance* means *beforehand.*

Agenda

> An *agenda* usually shows date, time and venue as well as all the items for discussion.

Venue:

> The *venue* is the place where the meeting is held.

Participants:

> The *participants* are the people attending the meeting. It is usual to include the names or initials of the participants.

Apologies

> The first item on the agenda is usually apologies from people who can't attend.

Minutes of last meeting

> The *minutes* are a summary of the points discussed and agreed at the meeting. The chairperson usually circulates the minutes of the last meeting to everyone who was present:
> *I'm attaching the minutes of the last meeting.*
> *Here are the minutes of Friday's meeting.*

AOB

> *AOB* stands for *any other business.* This is always the last item on the agenda to discuss any other issues.

Date of next meeting

> Note how the article *the* can be left out when writing in note form:
> *(The) Minutes of (the) last meeting.*
> *(The) Sales projections for (the) next quarter.*

Please note the change to item 2 on the agenda ...

> An agenda for a meeting has *items* (subjects) which are discussed.
> *Please note* is a formal way to point out changes. You could also say:
> *Please note that item 2 on the agenda has now changed.*

... I have moved the International Strategies paper to next week.

> Items on the agenda can be *moved.* Other verbs to use with agenda are:
> *Please advise if you want to <u>make</u> any amendments to the agenda.*
> *There is a <u>change</u> to item 3 on the agenda.*
> *Could you <u>draft</u> an agenda for Friday's meeting?*

She will circulate these to everyone prior to the meeting.

> *To circulate papers* is to pass papers around to everyone.
> *Prior to is* a formal expression for *before.*

... our computer system is down ...

> *To be down* is an expression which means *not working* when used for computers.

Is it possible to put this on the agenda for Monday's meeting?

> You could also say:
> *Is there any chance of putting this on the agenda for Monday's meeting?*
> *Would it be possible to discuss this at Monday's meeting?*

I'd like to run through the final arrangements ...

> *To run through* something is to look at the details to make sure you are familiar with everything. You could also say:
> *Let's go through all the final arrangements.*
> *Let's go over the final arrangements for tomorrow.*

... we need to ensure that everything runs smoothly.

> *To run smoothly* is to work without any problems.

British/American differences

British	American
venue	place/location
Apologies	present or absent
AOB:	Other/Unfinished business
item	topic
staff induction day	new employee orientation day

Meeting follow-up

Minutes of a Meeting

<u>Minutes of Marketing Managers Meeting</u>
<u>Friday 6th April</u>
<u>Conference Room C</u>

<u>Present:</u>   Don Room (Chair), Yu Liang, Martina Lenka, John Dawes, Doris Gonzalez, Jo Dent
<u>Apologies:</u>   Jamie Johns

		Action by	*Completion Date*
1	**Review of last quarter's performance**		
	Sales up by 25 per cent.		
	All teams to provide weekly report to DR.	YL/ML/DG	ongoing
2	*Marketing Activity*		
	(i) Trip to Czech Republic May 13–19.		
	Briefing to team – 24th May 10 a.m. Room C1.	ML	24th May
	(ii) New brochure ready for distribution on 8th April.	JJ	8th April
3	*Targets*		
	Target for next quarter – aim for 30 per cent increase in sales.		
	Schedule interviews with Press to publicise success.	DR	end April
4	*AOB*		
	Congratulations to marketing team on excellent performance this quarter.		

Next Meeting: 13th April 11 a.m. Conference Room C

Suggested amendments

Dear Don

I've just looked at the minutes and realised that I'll be out of the country again on the 24th. **We'll need to rearrange a date** for my briefing to the team. **I suggest the 2nd June. Can you please send out an amendment to everyone,** if this date suits you?
Sorry about this.
Martina

Comments

Don,
Sorry I couldn't make today's meeting. **Re. the new brochures** (item 2ii); I've just heard from the printers that there has been a problem with the machine, so we're expecting a delay of about three days. They will still be ready in time for Martina's trip. **By the way,** they look great!
I was interested to see our new sales target for next quarter too. We'll have a busy few weeks!
Jamie

Thanks

Don
Thanks for your comments on our performance this quarter. **I've passed on your congratulations to the team.** Everyone has worked very hard. **Thank you for all your support** during the past few weeks.
Liang

Notes

Action by

The minutes usually name the person who will carry out the actions discussed. A completion date (date by which something must be done) is also usually given.

Review of last quarter's performance

This is looking back at the company's activities during the past three months.
Note also:
Preview of next quarter is looking forward at what will happen over the next three months.

All teams to provide weekly report ...

Writing in note form (leaving out verbs, articles, etc.) is common in minutes.
Brochure to be ready by 8th April.
Congratulations to marketing team.
Press Officer to contact local media.

Briefing ...

This is a meeting at which information or instructions are given.
There will be a briefing meeting at 2 p.m.
Could all managers please attend the team briefing this afternoon?

Schedule interviews with Press ...

To schedule is to *arrange a date*.
Please schedule the meeting for Friday.
Can you schedule the interviews for next week?

I've just looked at the minutes ...

Just is a useful way to start a memo or email. See also:
I've just read your report.
I've just seen the latest figures.

We'll need to rearrange a date ...

You could also say:
Can we set a new date?
Can we rearrange the briefing for next Monday?

I suggest the 2nd June.

This is a formal way of making a suggestion. More informally, you could say:
What about 2nd June?
Let's change it to 2nd June.

Can you please send out an amendment to everyone, ...

An *amendment* is a *change*.

Re. the new brochures ...

Re. means *with reference to* and is short for *regarding*. (See also the appendix on page 95 for common abbreviations.)

By the way, ...

Here *by the way* is used to give further information. It can also be used to introduce a new subject:
The figures are very impressive. By the way, when is the next project meeting?

I was interested to see our new sales target ...

Note also:
It was interesting to see our new sales target ...
I understand from the minutes that we have a new sales target ...

Thanks for your comments on ...

More formally:
I appreciate your comments on ...
I am very grateful for your comments on ...

I've passed on your congratulations to the team.

To pass something on means to give someone a message or information from someone else.
I'll pass on your thanks.
Could you pass on the message to him please?

Thank you for all your support ...

Support means *help*. For example:
Your support is greatly appreciated.
Thank you for supporting me.

Practice

1 **Choose a word from the box to complete each sentence.**

available	manage	availability	suits	suit	~~best~~

EXAMPLE: Which is . . *best* . . . for you, the 14th, 15th or 16th February?

a Can you let me know your . . . . next week?

b Can you . . . . 2 p.m. tomorrow?

c Would 12th January . . . . you?

d When are you . . . . ?

e That . . . . me.

2 **Select an appropriate phrase to begin each sentence.**

We'll need to	Can you confirm	Thank you for	Can you pass on

~~I am looking forward~~	Please let me know	What about	I would be very pleased

EXAMPLE: . *I am looking forward* . . to meeting you on Friday.

1 . . . . circulate the meeting notes.

2 . . . . all your help during the project.

3 . . . . my congratulations to everyone?

4 . . . . the date of the meeting?

5 . . . . if you want to make any changes.

6 . . . . to visit you next week.

7 . . . . meeting for lunch tomorrow?

3 **Match the words with the correct definition.**

1	to brief	i	To send information to a number of people.
2	item	ii	The place where an event takes place.
3	minutes	iii	To give someone the information they need to do their work.
4	agenda	iv	A specified time during the meeting when a specific subject can be discussed.
5	participant	v	One of the subjects to be discussed at a meeting.
6	venue	vi	An official written record of what is said at a meeting.
7	circulate	vii	Someone who takes part in a meeting or conference.
8	slot	viii	A list of the subjects to be discussed at a meeting.

4 Complete the puzzle below and find the keyword.

1 Can I have a copy of the *agenda* . . . . before the meeting?

2 I'm afraid he's not *a* . . . . on Monday.

3 How many *P* . . . . were at the conference?

4 I think I'm free. I'll look in my *d* . . . .

5 I can't make Monday's meeting now. We'll have to *r* . . . .

6 We'll need to make some *a* . . . . to the minutes before I send them out.

7 Can you *b* . . . . me on the American market?

8 Can you take the *m* . . . . of today's meeting, John?

9 Sarah can't be here today – she sends her *a* . . . .

10 There's been a change to the first *i* . . . . on the agenda.

11 Sandy, can you *c* . . . . the meeting notes to everybody please?

12 Paul, can you give us a quick *s* . . . . of progress so far?

  KEYWORD = *a* . . . .

5 Use the note and diary page below to write a short email to all staff in the Marketing Department. Write about thirty words, using the language and notes in the unit to help you.

M e s s a g e

For: Pierre   From: Hank   Date: Friday 10th May

Pierre,
Can you organise a meeting with all Marketing staff, and email everyone to tell them the details?

- Date – Tuesday 14th May
- Time – look at my diary for the best time – we'll need 2 hours
- Subject – to discuss our new brochure
- Venue – conference room

Thanks – See you when I get back from Amsterdam.

Diary   Tuesday 14

09:00	Meeting with Jacques until 11:00
10:00	
11:00	
12:00	Lunch with Nicole – until 14:00
14:00	
16:00	Taxi to airport
18:00	Flight KL1058 Amsterdam

Subject: _____

▷ Attachments: *none*

To all Marketing Staff

. . . .

. . . .

. . . .

. . . .

. . . .

. . . .

. . . .

. . . .

. . . .

. . . .

6 Complete the sentences with a suitable preposition.

EXAMPLE: Can you put this . . .on. . . the agenda please?

a   There will be a Health and Safety meeting . . . . Pieter Godoy's office . . . . 3:15 tomorrow.

b   The next Senior Management team meeting will be . . . . 10:00 a.m. . . . . Wednesday May 18.

c   All agenda items . . . . the meeting . . . . Monday 26 should reach me . . . . Thursday 22.

d   I want to meet . . . . . . all Department Heads . . . . the Port Vale Site tomorrow . . . . . . 8:00 a.m.

e   Please let me know . . . . advance if you want to make any changes.

f   I would like to brief you all . . . . the latest situation . . . . Germany.

5 Enquiries

Some useful phrases.

We are looking for a new supplier.
We are very interested in your new range of products.
Please send us a current price list.

Thank you for your interest in our products.
I have attached a copy of our latest company brochure.
I will send you a copy of our new catalogue.
You will find further information on our website.
Please have a look at our website.

We are having problems with the new machine.
What would you advise us to do?
Who would you recommend?

Sorry to hear about your problems.
Have you thought about contacting EFPC?
I can strongly recommend them.
It's a very reliable company.
You could also contact Universal Tools.

Messages 1

A general enquiry

Dear Sir/Madam
We are looking for a new supplier of healthcare products and your company has been recommended to us. **Please send me a current price list,** together with information on delivery times and costs. We would be grateful if you could include **some samples**.
Best regards
Paulo Sambucco

A reply

Dear Mr Sambucco
Thank you for your interest in our products. **Your email was forwarded to me** by our colleagues in Sweden. We offer a wide range of products, all based on natural materials and **we believe in buying from Fairtrade organisations.**

You will find further information on our website. Please email me your postal address and **I will send you a copy of our new catalogue.** We have local representatives and I would be happy to arrange a visit.
I look forward to hearing from you.
Yours sincerely

Francesca Maurois

A further request

Dear Ms Maurois
Many thanks for your prompt response to my enquiry. Your catalogue arrived yesterday. Would it be possible for one of your representatives to visit us? **We are very interested in ordering from you** but there are a number of things which we would like to discuss face-to-face.
Best regards
Paulo Sambucco

A reply

Dear Mr Sambucco
Thank you for requesting a visit from one of our representatives. Eva Gaveaux, our senior sales manager will be in Italy during the last two weeks of May. **Would May 24th be a suitable time to visit you?** If not, perhaps you could suggest some alternatives.
Looking forward to hearing from you.
Francesca Maurois

A cover note

With compliments

As requested, I enclose a copy of our latest company brochure. Please let me know if you require any further information.
Regards
Francesca Maurois

Notes

Please send me a current price list, ...

Some common phrases for requesting information:
Can you (please) send us information about ...
Could you (please) send a list of your products ...
Can you let us have more details.

... some samples.

Samples are examples of products.

Thank you for your interest in our products.

Other responses to an enquiry or request:
Thank you for requesting information about ...
Thank you for your enquiry about ...
Thank you for enquiring about ...

Your email was forwarded to me ...

To forward (formal) means *to send on* or *pass on.* Useful expressions:
I will pass on your message.
Your letter was sent on to me.
Please forward this message to the appropriate department (formal)

... we believe in buying from Fairtrade organisations.

Note the use of the *–ing* form after *to believe in, insist on, be interested in, to be good at.*
Examples:
We insist on buying from local producers.
We are very interested in doing business with your company.
The company is good at dealing with problems.

Fairtrade organisations are organisations which literally 'trade fairly' by doing business directly with the producers of goods, especially from developing countries.

You will find further information on our website.

Other phrases for referring to the web:
More details are available on the website.
You can find out more by logging on to our website.
Our website address is www.zp.net.wld
Visit our website at ...

... I will send you a copy of our new catalogue.

Responding to a request:
I'll send you our brochure.

I'll make sure you receive our catalogue.
I'll post it today.

Many thanks for your prompt response ...

Alternatives:
Many thanks for your quick response.
Thanks for getting back to me so quickly.

We are very interested in ordering from you ...

Note again the use of *-ing* after *interested in.*

Would May 24th be a suitable time to visit you?

Some alternatives:
Does Thursday suit you?
What is the best time for you?
Would May 24th be OK? (informal)

... I enclose a copy of our latest company brochure.

Some useful phrases for cover notes:
I have enclosed the report.
The report is enclosed.
Herewith the information you requested.

British/American differences

British	American
postal address	mailing address
enquiry/inquiry	Note: *enquiry/inquiry* exists in American English but is not often used.
catalogue	catalog
A compliments slip	Note: this expression is not used in American English; employees often have memo pads printed with their names (From the desk of Jane Doe) to use for short notes.
I'll post it today.	I'll mail it today.
Would 24th May be OK? (Pronounced the twenty-fourth of May)	Would May 24th be OK? (Pronounced May twenty-fourth)
Does Thursday suit you?	Is Thursday OK with you? (also used in British English)

Messages 2

Specific enquiries

Dear Bill

We are having problems with the new machine that you installed for us in the New Year. Every time we run the machine for more than four hours it overheats. Our engineers have followed all the instructions in the manual but there is no improvement. **What would you advise us to do?**

By the way, do you know where can we obtain parts for our DCI equipment? Our handbook doesn't list local suppliers. **Are there any that you can recommend?**

Many thanks
Lee

Advice and recommendations

Dear Lee

Sorry to hear about your problems. I'd like to send one of our engineers to your factory before offering any advice. He should be with you by 10 a.m. tomorrow. In the meantime, **it's best not to start the machine again until he arrives.**

As for the parts – **have you considered contacting Gudul?** We have used them a lot and I can strongly recommend them. Their delivery times are good and they are very reliable. Also **you could contact Universal Tools** – their number is 604934.

Best regards

Bill

A request for information

Dear Sir/Madam,

I have visited your website www.english4.co.uk and **I would be grateful if you could send me further information** about your courses. I would like to attend a general business English course starting in February. If you do not offer a suitable course at this time, please recommend an alternative. I studied English for five years at school and three years at university.

Best wishes

Jose Sanchez

Forwarding a request

Dear Jose
Thank you for your enquiry. I'm afraid we do not run any general business English **courses** in February. I have forwarded your enquiry to Filton College which runs courses throughout the year.
Best regards
Milrisa Lerte

Providing details

Dear Jose

With reference to your enquiry, I have attached a copy of our brochure. **You can see further details of our school by going to our website.** Please contact me if you have any questions.

Regards

Vera Baxter

Notes

What would you advise us to do?

Alternatives:
What is your advice?
Can you advise us?
Do you have any advice?
Note the spelling: verb –s; noun –c.
Also: *practise* (v); *practice* (n).

You will also see *advise* used to mean *tell, let us know, inform.* Examples are:
Please advise us when you arrive.
I'll advise you as soon as I know.

By the way, ...

This is a useful informal phrase for introducing a new topic.
By the way, I will be visiting DCI next week.

Are there any that you can recommend?

Other uses of *recommend:*
Who would you recommend?
I can strongly recommend Gudul.
They are highly recommended.
My recommendation is ...
We recommend using ...

... it's best not to start the machine again until he arrives.

You could also write:
(Please) don't start the machine until he arrives.
We don't recommend starting the machine until the engineer arrives.

... have you considered contacting Gudul?

Use the *-ing* form after *consider:*
We considered buying from Roxo.
We have considered using them.

... you could contact Universal Tools ...

Other ways to make suggestions:
Why don't you try Universal Tools.
What about trying Universal Tools?
I suggest contacting ...

... I would be grateful if you could send me further information ...

This is a polite phrase for making requests.
Also: *Please send me ...*
Could you please send me ...

Thank you for your enquiry.

Other phrases: *Thank you for contacting us.*
Thank you for your interest in our company.

I'm afraid we do not run any (...) courses

You can use *I'm afraid* as an alternative to *unfortunately* and *I'm sorry:*
I'm sorry but we don't run any courses.
Unfortunately we don't run any courses.

With reference to your enquiry, ...

The formal phrase *With reference to* is sometimes shortened to *Re.* and *With ref. to* in less formal contexts:
Re. your email.
With ref. to your enquiry.
However, it is more friendly to say simply:
Thank you for your enquiry.

You can see further details of our school by going to our website.

It is helpful to provide sources of further information:
Our website has further details.
Please refer to our brochure for further information.
Let me know if you need further details.

British/American differences

British	American
If you do not offer a suitable course.	*If you do not offer an appropriate program.*
I studied ... at school.	Note: *School* in American English refers to all levelsof education. *Where did you go to school?* generally refers to the highest level you completed, usually college or university. Americans say college, even if the institution they attend is a university.
practise (not used in American English)	*practice* (for both verb and noun)

Practice

1 Complete the sentences with a preposition.

EXAMPLE: Many thanks .*for*. your prompt reply.

a   I have put some information . . . . . the post.

b   We believe . . . . . buying from local suppliers.

c   We are looking . . . . . a new supplier.

d   I have forwarded your enquiry . . . . . BMES.

e   Where can we buy spare parts . . . . . our machinery?

f   I am interested . . . . . your new range of furniture.

g   . . . . . reference . . . . . your enquiry, I have attached our latest brochure.

2 Write the correct form of the verb with , -ing or infinitive with to, in these sentences.

EXAMPLE: We insist on .*buying*. . . . (buy) from local producers.

a   Sorry . . . . (hear) about all your problems.

b   It's best not . . . . (start) the process until everyone is ready.

c   Mr Roulins expects . . . . (be) in Boston next week.

d   She plans . . . . (arrive) early in the evening.

e   Our staff are good at . . . . (solve) problems.

f   We are interested in . . . . (buy) from Fairtade organisations.

g   We recommend . . . . (use) Gudul.

h   Thank you for . . . . (get) back to me so quickly.

i   You can find further details by . . . . (go) to our website.

3 Write these sentences in another way. Refer back to the messages in this unit.

EXAMPLE: You will find further information on our website.

For further information, .*refer to our website*. . . . .

a   I have posted you some information.

Some information is in . . . .

b   I have attached the report.

The report is . . . .

c   What would you advise?

What is . . . .?

d   EDR is strongly recommended by our company.

   Our company strongly . . . .

e   You could try closing the system down first.

   What about . . . . ?

f   I'm afraid we do not arrange delivery.

   I'm . . . . we do not arrange delivery,

4 Which sentence in each pair is the more informal? Tick ✓ the correct sentence.

a i Further to our discussion this morning, your payment will arrive at the end of the week. ☐
   ii As I said earlier, we're going to pay you at the end of the week. ✓

b i Please find attached a copy of our handbook. ☐
   ii I've attached a copy of our handbook. ☐

c i I have pleasure in advising you that we shall have a stand at the exhibition. ☐
   ii I'm pleased to say that we are going to have a stand at the exhibition. ☐

d i Please contact me if there are any other problems. ☐
   ii Please do not hesitate to contact me if there are any other problems. ☐

e i I am writing to advise you that our representative will visit you next month. ☐
   ii Just to let you know that our representative will visit you next month. ☐

f i I have been considering the Inko offer and believe that we should accept it. ☐
   ii I think we should accept the Inko offer. ☐

g i Please send me the report on Fairtrade. ☐
   ii I would be grateful if you could send me the report on Fairtrade. ☐

5 Match the two parts of the sentences used in making enquiries.

1   I'd like to know   a   some more information about our products.
2   We are having problems   b   to our brochure.
3   We can recommend   c   arranging a suitable delivery date.
4   We are looking   d   you could send us more information.
5   I'll send you   e   where we can buy spare parts.
6   Please refer   f   a supplier in London.
7   We would like to arrange   g   on your website.
8   We would be grateful if   h   for a new supplier.
9   I couldn't find the information i   a visit.

6 Order the sentences into a response to an enquiry.

Enquiry 1

a   I have attached a copy of our latest catalogue. ☐

b   Thank you for your enquiry ☑

c   For the most up-to-date prices and offers, ☐

d   As requested, ☐

e   It contains all the information you need ☐

f   concerning prices and terms of delivery. ☐

g   I look forward to hearing from you soon. ☐

h   visit our website at www.efpc.co.uk. ☐

Enquiry 2

a   please contact Mr Jan Juoma. ☐

b   You asked about our new range of equipment ☐

c   If you are interested in a demonstration, ☐

d   Thank you for your interest in our company. ☑

e   and I enclose our brochure. ☐

f   I look forward to hearing from you. ☐

g   His email address is: j.juoma@dry.foo.net. ☐

7 Complete the sentences with a form of the word in brackets.

EXAMPLE: With . reference . . . . to your email.   (refer)

a   Have you considered . . . . John about it?   (contact)

b   I'd be interested in your . . . .   (recommend)

c   What is your . . . . ?   (advise)

d   Thank you for your . . . .   (enquire)

e   We need to find a more . . . . supplier.   (rely)

f   Find out more by . . . . on to our website.   (log)

g   I have . . . . a copy of our brochure.   (attach)

h   Your message was . . . . to us.   (forward)

6 Orders, dealing with problems

Some useful phrases.

We would like to order some items from your catalogue.
Could you please send us a quote?
Please confirm that the items are in stock.
Your terms and conditions state a delivery time of four weeks.

Thank you for your order.
I confirm that all the items you ordered are in stock.
We will deliver them within one week.
There is no additional charge for special delivery.
Your usual discount applies.

I'm sorry that we cannot meet the agreed schedule.
Our suppliers are having some problems.
I was very surprised to receive your message.
You promised us that the schedule was guaranteed.
This is very inconvenient.

We have still not received our order.
Could you let us know what is happening?

NO, THERE'S NO ADDITIONAL CHARGE FOR SPECIAL DELIVERY!

Orders

Requesting a quote

Dear Rona

We have recently ordered some new office furniture which will arrive on 24 July. **Could you please quote for**:

- **removal of existing furniture**
- assembly of new furniture (see attached list)
- disposal of all packaging

I estimate that this will be no more than a day's work for two people.

With thanks

Karim

Placing a first order

Dear Sir

We would like to place an order with you for the items listed on page 2 of your catalogue. Please confirm as soon as possible that these are all in stock.

Your terms and conditions state a delivery time of four weeks. Would it be possible to dispatch items 1 – 3 within two weeks as we need them urgently? If there is **an additional charge**, please let us know.

Yours faithfully

Jerome Gilbert (Purchasing assistant)

A reply

Dear Mr Gilbert

Thank you for your order. **I can confirm that all the items you ordered are in stock** and that we will deliver the items within two weeks. There will be no extra charge for delivery.

With best regards

Brad Askew
Sales Manager

Placing a repeat order

Zhou

How are you? We're pleased to say that sales of the Alio range have been very good and **we'd like a repeat order** for the following:

Alio   3 207 = **4 000pcs**

Alio   3 215 = 2 000pcs

I'm also interested in ordering 3 000 items from the Alia range which are in **your latest catalogue. Could you give us a firm delivery date** in early July and **confirm that our usual discount would apply?**

Best regards

Alima

Notes

We have recently ordered some new office furniture …

A more formal phrase for starting this message:
With reference to our recent order for new office furniture …

Could you please quote for:

A *quote* is an estimate. Asking for estimates of cost:
Could you give us a price for …
How much is it going to cost?
Please let me have a written quote.

removal of existing furniture

Note that items listed in a quotation are usually written in note form. Articles *(the, a/an)* are left out.

We would like to place an order with you …

To place an order means to order. Other verbs used with the noun *order:*
To change an order, cancel an order, confirm an order, to order again, to re-order

Your terms and conditions state a delivery time of four weeks.

Terms and conditions include price, method of payment, delivery times etc.

Would it be possible to dispatch items 1 – 3 within two weeks …

To dispatch is a formal term for *to send.*
We will dispatch your order on receipt of payment. (formal)
We will send your order as soon as we receive payment. (informal)

… an additional charge …

An additional charge is an *extra charge.*
Other expressions relating to charges:
There is no charge.
At no extra cost.
Free of charge.
It's included in the price.
A fixed charge. (The price is always the same.)

I can confirm that all the items you ordered are in stock …

In stock means that the items ordered are available and ready to send out.
The opposite is: *out of stock*
The chairs you ordered are currently out of stock. We should have some next week.

… we'd like a repeat order …

This means that the order is exactly the same as the previous order.

4 000pcs

Pcs is an abbreviation for *pieces.*
(See page 00 for more abbreviations)

… your latest catalogue.

This is the most recent, the most up-to-date catalogue.

Could you give us a firm delivery date …

Firm means definite, fixed.
Delivery date is when goods should arrive.
The date of dispatch is the day the goods leave the supplier.
Delivery time is the length of time between receiving the order and sending the goods.
To take delivery of is to receive the goods.

(Could you) confirm that our usual discount would apply?

You can also say:
Please confirm that we would receive our usual discount.
A discount is a reduced price:
What kind of discount can you offer?
Our usual discount is 15 per cent.

British/American differences

British	American
quote	quotation/estimate (*estimate* is also used in British English)
Yours faithfully	Yours truly/Sincerely
To dispatch/ despatch	To ship/send out (also used in British English)

Dealing with problems 1

Problems with a schedule

Dear Mr Bassos

I'm sorry to say that we may not be able to meet the agreed schedule. Our usual supplier is experiencing difficulties and has warned us that there is a five-week waiting list for delivery of materials. I'm afraid **we will fall behind schedule** if we cannot find an alternative supplier.

Yours

Brenda Hind

A reply

Dear Ms Hind

I was very surprised to receive your message. You assured us that this schedule was guaranteed and there would be no problems keeping to it. Please try to find an alternative supplier of materials so that that there will be no delays.

Yours truly,

Dmitri Bassos

Damaged goods

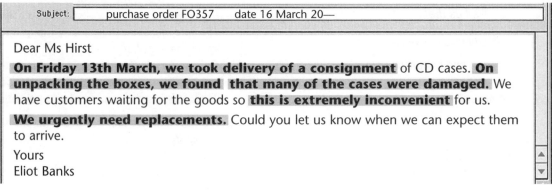

Subject: purchase order FO357   date 16 March 20—

Dear Ms Hirst

On Friday 13th March, we took delivery of a consignment of CD cases. **On unpacking the boxes, we found that many of the cases were damaged.** We have customers waiting for the goods so **this is extremely inconvenient** for us.

We urgently need replacements. Could you let us know when we can expect them to arrive.

Yours
Eliot Banks

A reply

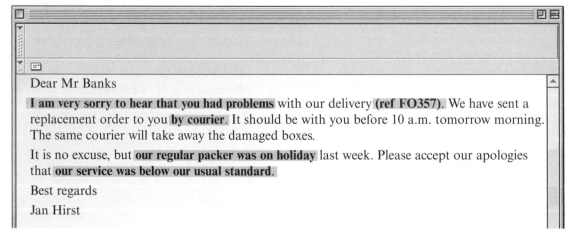

Dear Mr Banks

I am very sorry to hear that you had problems with our delivery **(ref FO357).** We have sent a replacement order to you **by courier.** It should be with you before 10 a.m. tomorrow morning. The same courier will take away the damaged boxes.

It is no excuse, but **our regular packer was on holiday** last week. Please accept our apologies that **our service was below our usual standard.**

Best regards

Jan Hirst

Notes

I'm sorry to say that we may not be able to meet the agreed schedule.

Note the use of *sorry* here:
I'm/I was sorry to hear about it.
I'm sorry (that) we cannot meet the schedule.
I'm sorry to tell/inform you that …

In the sentence *to meet the agreed schedule*, *to meet* means *to keep to*.

… we will fall behind schedule …

Other expressions:
We will be late.
We will miss the deadline.
The goods will be delayed.

I was very surprised to receive your message.

Notice how, for the sake of keeping good relations with the supplier at this stage, the writer uses *surprised* rather than *annoyed* or *angry*.

You assured us that this schedule was guaranteed …

Other phases:
You guaranteed the schedule.
You gave us your word that you would keep to the schedule.
You promised us that you could meet the schedule.

On Friday 13th March we took delivery of a consignment …

Note that we *take delivery* of goods.
When the goods arrive we can *sign for them*.

On unpacking the boxes, we found …

On unpacking the boxes means as soon as/ when we unpacked the boxes.
On opening the boxes, we saw …
On reading the instructions, I noticed …

… that many of the cases were damaged.

Some common complaints!
The goods arrived late.
The goods were sent to the wrong address.

… this is extremely inconvenient …

Other phrases:
It was very inconvenient.
It has caused us a lot of inconvenience.
This is a great inconvenience for us.

We urgently need replacements.

Other requests:
We need them immediately.
We would like a refund.
We want our money back.

I am very sorry to hear that you had problems …

The writer apologises and puts things right.
I'm very sorry about this.
I'm sorry, it was my fault.
I will sort it out immediately.

(ref. FO357)

Ref. is short for *reference* (number)
See other abbreviations on page 95.

… by courier.

By courier means that the goods will be sent quickly by an express delivery company.
By express means by express delivery.
By return means sent immediately after receipt of a letter/order.

… our regular packer was on holiday …

Other possible reasons why the problem happened:
The computer system was down.
There was a fire in the building.
We have had a staff shortage.
A lot of staff have been off sick.

… our service was below our usual standard.

Below our usual standard means not as good as usual/not up to our usual standard.

British/American differences	
British	**American**
the agreed schedule	the schedule we agreed on
on holiday	on vacation
apologise	apologize

Dealing with problems 2

Unacceptable service

Dear Mr Dennis

We are very unhappy with the level of service you have given us this year. Your service engineers never arrive within the promised 24 hours and **we always have to wait for spare parts.** As a result **we have had to shut down production on three occasions.** I'd like to meet you to discuss how things can improve in the future.

Yours sincerely

Catherine Easterbrook

Reply

Dear Ms Easterbrook

Thank you for your letter. **I was very sorry to hear about the problems you have experienced.** I have forwarded your letter to our customer service manager asking him for a full report. We should meet as soon as I hear **the outcome** of his investigations. **I expect to receive his report by the end of this week.**

Yours sincerely

Martin Dennis

Misleading information

Subject: Order no 908

Dear Sir

We have still not received this order. It says on your website that you will deliver within three days and it is now five days since we placed the order. Could you let us know what is happening.

Chris Moran

Reply

Dear Mr Moran

We are very sorry that you have not yet received your order and **we apologise for any misunderstanding** caused by the information on our website. Delivery to addresses outside Europe normally take five days. **We do try** to keep our website up-to-date and I have discussed this matter with our website manager.

Your sincerely

Peter Wieser

Rejecting a complaint

Dear Ms Ono

With reference to your complaint re order no. 376, our quality control staff have tested all the goods you sent back to us. **I regret that we cannot accept the return as faulty goods** since they meet all our quality standards. However, as **a goodwill gesture,** we will accept them as unwanted goods and will issue **a credit note. I trust this meets with your approval.**

Yours sincerely

Sergio da Silva (Customer service)

Notes

We are very unhappy with the level of service ...

Some strong complaints:
We were very dissatisfied with ...
Your level of service is unsatisfactory.
These delays are totally unacceptable.

... we always have to wait for spare parts.

Note the position of *always,* and other time
expressions such as: *never, rarely,
occasionally, often, usually etc.* in a sentence:
The sales department rarely answer the phone.
The goods never arrive on time.
We often need to remind you.

**... we have had to shut down production on
three occasions.**

Phrases such as *on three occasions, every
month* etc. can come at the beginning or end
of the sentence:
On four occasions we have had to shut down ...
Every month we have problems.
We have problems every month.

**I was very sorry to hear about the problems you
have experienced.**

Less formal: *I was very sorry to hear about the
problems you've had.*

... the outcome ...

An *outcome* is the result (of a process).
*I do not know the outcome of the investigations
yet.*

**I expect to receive his report by the end of this
week.**

Should can be used instead of *expect to* or
hope to:
I should receive the report by Wednesday.
I'm hoping to receive it by Wednesday.
I should hear from them tomorrow.
I expect to hear from them tomorrow.

We have still not received this order.

Problems with deliveries:
We are still waiting for the delivery.
The delivery is now two days late.
We need it urgently.

... we apologise for any misunderstanding ...

Note that we apologise *for* something.
The expressions *We apologise for/Please
accept our apologies* are more formal than
We are sorry. Other formal phases for
apologising: *I sincerely apologise for ...*
My sincere apologies.

We do try...

Do/does are added for emphasis, especially
when there is disagreement.
We do need to improve our service.
The terms and conditions do state ...

**I regret that we cannot accept the return as
faulty goods ...**

Note how we use *regret* to express a polite
rejection:
I regret that we cannot deliver on Sundays.
Polite but less formal:
I'm afraid we can't accept ...
I'm sorry but we can't deliver ...

... a goodwill gesture, ...

A *goodwill gesture* is a friendly and helpful
action which is good for maintaining
business relations.

... a credit note.

If goods are faulty they can be returned to
the supplier and a *credit note* is issued. This
document informs the customer of the
money owed for the faulty goods.

I trust this meets with your approval.

This is a formal expression. Note also:
I trust this is satisfactory.
To be less formal, use: *I hope this helps.*
I hope you are happy with this.

British/American differences

British	American
The sales department rarely answer the phone.	*The sales department rarely answers the phone.* Note: American English treats company and departmental names as singular.
a credit note	*a credit receipt/ a credit slip*

Practice

1 Choose the best alternative.

EXAMPLE: We have still not *taken/left/received* the order.

a   We will send you a replacement *order/enquiry/service*.

b   Could you *change/check/forward* the original message to me.

c   You *believed/assured/said* us that the schedule was guaranteed.

d   Please *accept/make/take* our apologies.

e   Your order will be *quoted/damaged/dispatched* on Monday of next week.

f   I'm sorry we can't *meet/take/find* the schedule.

2 Complete the sentences with a preposition

EXAMPLE: I am writing to complain . about . the last two orders you sent us.

a   We are trying to keep . . . . the schedule.

b   Unfortunately the goods did not arrive. . . . . time.

c   We would like to place an order. . . . . two machines.

d   Please let me know if you have any problems . . . . this.

e   The cases should arrive . . . . 3 p.m. on Friday at the latest.

f   We apologise . . . . the misunderstanding.

g   I am sorry that we cannot give you a refund . . . . this occasion.

h   We are still waiting . . . . the delivery to arrive.

i   We are very happy . . . . the service you have given us. Many thanks!

3 Match the two parts of the sentences.

1	We need the goods	a	me if there are any problems.
2	I was very sorry to hear	b	for all the inconvenience.
3	I'm sorry that	c	not clear enough.
4	I'm arranging	d	your letter to our Head Office.
5	Please phone	e	urgently.
6	I sincerely apologise	f	about the problems you have had.
7	I have forwarded	g	for an express delivery of your order.
8	I hope	h	I cannot be more helpful.
9	Unfortunately the information was	i	you are happy with this

4 **The eight sentences below are part of a company's response to a letter of complaint. Complete each sentence with a verb from the box.**

showed	have experienced	to discuss	to receive
have sent	return	~~letting~~	will refund	apologise

EXAMPLE: Thank you for .letting. . . us know about the problems you had with the delivery.

a We apologise for the difficulties you . . . .

b We need . . . . how we can improve our service in the future,

c I expect . . . . a report from dispatch department tomorrow.

d This morning we . . . . you a new consignment by next day delivery.

e Please . . . . the faulty goods to us and we . . . . the delivery cost.

f Once again, we . . . . for any inconvenience caused.

5 **Match the words in the box with the words which have similar meanings in the sentences.**

additional	definite	concerned	promise	a refund
dissatisfied	~~most recent~~	dispatch	a discount	meet

EXAMPLE: Thank you for sending me your *latest*/.most recent. .brochure.

a We were very *unhappy*/ . . . . about the level of service we received.

b We will *send*/ . . . . your order tomorrow.

c There is no *extra*/ . . . . charge for this service.

d Can you give me a *firm*/ . . . . delivery date?

e Can you offer us a *reduced price*/ . . . . ?

f We are very *worried*/ . . . . that the delivery will be late.

g I can *assure*/ . . . . you that everything will be OK.

h The goods did not arrive so we would like *our money back*/ . . . .

i I'm afraid we cannot *keep to*/ . . . . the agreed schedule.

6 Read this letter of complaint from a customer and write a reply.

> Dear Sir or Madam
>
> This morning we received a consignment of printers from you (Order no SN206). On unpacking the boxes, we noticed that all the printers were damaged.
>
> Could you please arrange to send a replacement order as soon as possible and arrange to collect the damaged goods? Hopefully, we will not have to pay for this.
>
> Yours faithfully
> Ms Janine Duval

Write a reply of 50 – 60 words to your customer:

- thanking her for her letter
- apologising for the problem
- agreeing to replace the damaged goods today
- offering to collect the damaged goods, at no extra cost

Use the texts and notes in this chapter to help you.

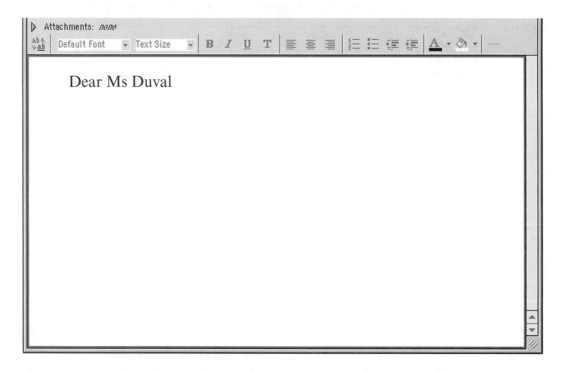

Some useful phrases.

Could you send me a short report?
The purpose of the visit was to appoint some new agents.
The visit was very successful.
There is one thing missing in the report.

66 per cent of our customers are satisfied with our products.
A third of our customers are not satisfied.
Spending rose by 8 per cent last year.
Costs went up from € 50 000 per year to € 76 000.

Sales rose substantially.
There was a sharp fall in sales.
The decline in sales is due to increased competition.
Profits rose in the last quarter.

What is your recommendation?
We recommend you should try a new supplier.
We suggest looking at some other companies.
You need to follow-up enquiries within three days.

Providing information

A request for information

Janet

Could you send me a short report on your recent Japan trip, in preparation for the next **Board meeting**? I'd appreciate this as soon as possible please.

Thanks

Simone

A short report

Japan Visit Report

Background

The purpose of the visit was to take part in the Tokyo Technology Exhibition and appoint new agents to help promote our products in the Far East.

Details

10 000 visitors attended the Tokyo Exhibition.

2 000 enquiries were received and 300 orders were placed.

2 new agents were appointed.

Actions / Recommendations

We need to follow up customer enquiries immediately.

We recommend that the new agents should visit the UK to see our production processes.

Conclusions

The visit was very successful, resulting immediately in new business worth over £300 000. Japan will be **a key market** for us for the future.

Report by Janet Robbins 14th October

Asking for missing information

Janet

Thanks for the visit report. **Just one thing missing – can you send me the cost analysis** showing total expenditure and anticipated income.

Thanks

Simone

Providing further information

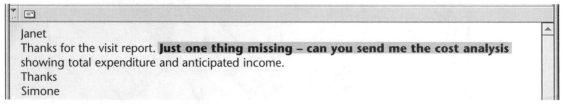

Cost Analysis
Expenditure

• **exhibition stand**	$ 10 500
• posting of catalogues	$ 2 200
• flights	$ 2 400
• accommodation	$ 3 600
• **expenses**	$ 3 700
• staffing	$ 6 000
Total **Expenditure**	$ 28 400
Anticipated Revenue	$ 400 000
Profit	$ 371 600

Notes

Could you send me a short report …

Could you is used to make a request.
You can also say:
Can you send me a short report?
Please email me a short report.

… Board meeting.

The Board is the group of Directors who manage the company.
We hold weekly Board meetings.
The members of the Board will hold a meeting.

Japan Visit Report

A formal or informal report has a clear title and sub-headings. The format varies depending on the purpose of the report and individual company style, but usually has the following sections:

Title
Background/Introduction
Details/Findings
Actions/Recommendations
Conclusions

The purpose of the visit was to take part in the Tokyo Technology Exhibition …

The opening sentence of a report clearly sets the scene:
This report shows sales from 2000 – 2003.
Finance requested a report on expenditure.

2 000 enquiries were received …

Use the passive to describe actions without saying who does them. For example:
Several complaints were received.
The restaurant was closed for two weeks.
200 new orders were placed today.

We need to follow up customer enquiries immediately.

Actions and recommendations often use verbs like *need, must, have to* and *should*:
We need to support our agents overseas.
We must make sure that we deliver today.
We must ensure our prices are competitive.

We recommend that the new agents should visit the UK …

When making a recommendation or suggestion, you could also say:

We recommend you try a new supplier.
We suggest looking at a number of alternatives.
Our recommendation is to sign the agreement.

… a key market …

A key market is a very important market for your products.

Just one thing missing – can you send me the cost analysis …

Use a dash (–) in an informal message to add a request or extra information.
More formally you could say:
There is just one thing missing.
Could you please send the cost analysis?

• exhibition stand $ 10 500

Bullet points (•) are often used when listing information, figures etc. to make the information clearer.

• expenses

The money given to you by your company to spend on company business.

… Expenditure

This is the amount of money spent. For example:
Marketing expenditure rose this year.

Anticipated Revenue

Anticipated is what you expect to happen.
Sales were higher than anticipated.
Revenue is the money the business receives from sales.
Revenue last year exceeded $35K.

British/American differences

British	American
exhibition stand	exhibition booth
posting of catalogues	mailing of catalogs
… as soon as possible.	ASAP (pronounced *ay-sap*) (This abbreviation is also used in British English – pronounced *ay-es-ay-pee* – but would only be used in informal emails.)

Focus on facts and figures

Presenting numbers

Visitor Feedback

This year we had over 25 000 visitors to the centre. **A third of the visitors were children** under sixteen. **Approximately 90 per cent of visitors said they found the centre informative** and interesting. **Most people were happy to pay the entrance fee of $3.50.**

Describing trends

Dear Marcia

You may be interested in the findings of our recent survey:

Findings

In the summer, we analysed the success of our new TV promotion by interviewing customers in different cities in Germany.

Following the TV promotion, **sales went up by 30 per cent**, in most major cities. In Hamburg, **there was a sharp rise of 40 per cent** from last year's figures. However, in the smaller cities, the promotion was less successful and **sales dropped slightly** by 2 per cent.

Making comparisons

Product Sales Report – First Quarter

Compared with last quarter, our supermarket **sales are higher.** Frozen foods are still our most popular product, with 52 per cent of total sales, followed by bread with 20 per cent and soft drinks with 10 per cent.

Drawing conclusions

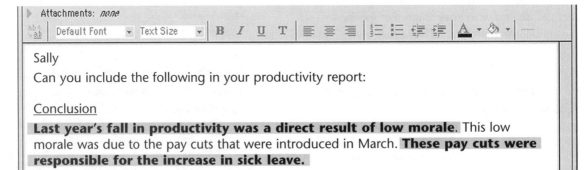

Attachments: *none*

| | Default Font | Text Size | **B** *I* <u>U</u> T | | | | | | | | | A | |

Sally

Can you include the following in your productivity report:

Conclusion

Last year's fall in productivity was a direct result of low morale. This low morale was due to the pay cuts that were introduced in March. **These pay cuts were responsible for the increase in sick leave.**

Jamie

Notes

This year we had over 25 000 visitors ...

Other ways of giving an approximate number:
We had more than 25 000 visitors.
There were about 25 000 visitors this year.
(*About* can mean more than or fewer than 25 000.)

A third of the visitors were children ...

A third = 33 per cent
A quarter = 25 per cent
A half = 50 per cent
Three quarters = 75 per cent

Approximately 90 per cent of the visitors said they found the centre informative ...

You can express figures as a percentage.
France has a 25 per cent market share.
40 per cent of our cars are exported.

Most people were happy to pay the entrance fee of $3.50.

In British English the decimal point is written as a dot (.). Many other countries use a comma (,).

... sales went up by 30 per cent, ...

Other verbs to describe an upward change:
Sales rose by 20 per cent.
Orders increased last month.
Sales peaked in June.
Note the use of the prepositions *by* and *to* in these sentences:
Consumer spending rose by 10 per cent last year.
Spending increased from 8 per cent to 10 per cent last year.

...there was a sharp rise of 40 per cent ...

Other adjectives to describe a change:
There has been a steady decline in enquiries.
There was a slight drop in sales last month.
There was a significant improvement in orders.
There was a dramatic rise in profits.

... sales dropped slightly ...

Other verbs to describe a downward change:
Profits went down last year.
Sales fell in January.

Orders declined last month.
Numbers decreased in July.
Slightly indicates a small change.
Other adverbs to describe the degree of change:
Sales fell significantly last month.
Orders declined steadily last quarter.
Profits went down dramatically.

... sales are higher.

When making comparisons you can use expressions such as:
Sales were higher in April than in May.
This model is more expensive than the old one.
Chocolate is our most popular product.
This is the least successful product.

Last year's fall in productivity was a direct result of low morale.

Alternatives to *a direct result of:*
It was a consequence of low morale.
It was due to low morale.
Morale is a mental and emotional condition of enthusiasm, confidence and loyalty.

These pay cuts were responsible for the increase in sick leave.

Alternatives to *to be responsible* for:
The pay cuts caused the increase ...
The pay cuts resulted in an increase ...

British/American differences

British	American
75% = three quarters	also: *a fourth; three fourths*
101 = one hundred and one	also: 101 = one hundred one
centre	center
Last year's fall in productivity.	Last year's drop in productivity. (also used in British English)
... an increase in sick leave. (*sick leave* not used in American English)	an increase in the number of sick days. (also used in British English)

Practice

1 **Look at the company sales report below. Decide in which part of the report (A – D) you would find the information (1 – 7).**

ITC plc   Sales Report

A   Introduction

....

B   Findings

   1 Sales worldwide rose by 18 per cent in the last quarter. ....

   ....

   ....

C   Recommendations

   ....

   ....

D   Conclusion

   ....

1	Sales worldwide rose by 18 per cent in the last quarter.
2	This report shows the breakdown of sales during the last year.
3	Europe still has the largest share of the market.
4	We need to increase our advertising in the Far East.
5	Overall, business was very good last year and we expect this success to continue.
6	Sales in the Far East fell by 3 per cent.
7	We must appoint new agents in the Far East.

2 **Underline the correct word to complete this report.**

Sales Report

Introduction

This report shows the sales trends for the last financial year.

Details

a   At the start of the year, there was a *steady/steadier* drop in sales.

b   However, there was a *sharp/sharply* increase in March.

c   This was *due to/caused/resulted* in the introduction of a new pricing policy.

d   Sales continued to rise steadily *in/on* April and May.
      The summer sales campaign was very successful.

e   This resulted in a dramatic *drop/increase* in sales during August.
      This trend continued until the end of the year.

Recommendations

f   We need to ensure our pricing policy is *compete/competition/competitive.*

g   We suggest *investing/invest* in further sales campaigns next year.

Conclusion

h   *In total/Overall*, this was a very successful year for us.

i   Compared with last year, sales were much *high/higher/highest.*

3 Put in an appropriate word or phrase from the box to complete the following report.

due	~~purpose~~	recommend	recommendation	visitors	placed

1 Introduction

The . . . . . *purpose* . . . . of the report is to analyse success of our marketing in Brazil.

2 Details

a 25 000 . . . . attended the Trade Fair in Sao Paolo.

b 900 enquiries were taken.

c 150 orders were . . . .

3 Recommendations

a The main . . . . is to appoint new agents in Brazil.

b We also . . . . opening an office in Sao Paolo.

c We need to make a decision by the end of the month.

4 Conclusion

The increase in business was . . . . to our new marketing strategy. Brazil will be a key market for us in the future.

4 Find 6 verbs in the square which show an upward or downward movement.

EXAMPLE: decrease

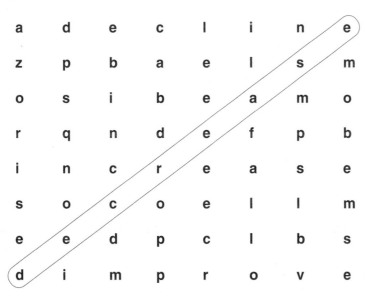

a	d	e	c	l	i	n	e
z	p	b	a	e	l	s	m
o	s	i	b	e	a	m	o
r	q	n	d	e	f	p	b
i	n	c	r	e	a	s	e
s	o	c	o	e	l	l	m
e	e	d	p	c	l	b	s
d	i	m	p	r	o	v	e

5 Look at the graphs below, then use the phrases in the box to complete the report.

Each paragraph has been started for you. Decide which graph each paragraph describes.

1 .... 2 .... 3 ....

| ~~successful~~ | ~~the least~~ | improvement | ~~rose~~ | drop |
| a sharp decline | resulted in | due to | very low |

Three years ago we opened three new shops.

A

Alpha performed well in the first year and sales . .rose. . . . . significantly.

However, a change of management in year two led to . . . .

Fortunately, a new manager was appointed last year and there has been a steady . . . . since then.

B

In the first year BNK was . . the least . . . . successful of the three stores. Sales were . . . . and did not improve much in the second year. Then we redesigned the store and this has . . . . a significant increase in sales.

C

In contrast, Geo was the most . successful . in year one. However, since then, sales have fallen . . . . increased competition locally.

Sales are continuing to . . . . and we may have to consider closing the store.

8 Personal messages

Some useful phrases.

Just a quick note to say many thanks for sorting out the problems.
We really appreciate everything you have done.
Many congratulations!
Well done!

This is to let you know that I will be leaving the company.
Please come and visit me.
It would be great to see you.
I was sorry to hear that you are leaving.
I wish you every success in the future.

Good news!
I've just received the results of the survey.
The results are very good.
You've done a great job!

Have you remembered about the party?
We hope you can make it.
Thanks for reminding me.
I'd love to come.

Messages 1

Appreciation

Hi Bill

Just a quick note to say many thanks for sorting out the problems with the deliveries last week. **We really appreciate everything you have done.**

Look forward to seeing you in Madrid next month.

All the best

Tina

Congratulations

Dear Florian

Many congratulations on your promotion. Everyone here in the Tripoli office has asked me to send you their best wishes. We'll miss your visits – **stay in touch.**

With best regards

Tareq

A personal announcement

Dear friends and colleagues

This is to let you know that I will be leaving EFPC at the end of this month. After a very enjoyable career in the Buenos Aires office I have decided to move back to Brazil. **Please come and visit me** if you are visiting Rio – you all have my mobile number!

With very best wishes

Mario

Saying goodbye

Dear Mario

I was very sorry to hear that you are leaving the company. It has been a pleasure working with you and **I wish you every success in the future**.

Best wishes, Alejandro

Saying thank you

Donna

Thanks for all your help during the conference in London last week. It went really well. We are planning another event in Dubai in March and we would really appreciate your help there. Let me know if you can make it. **It would be great to see you there.**

All the best

Ashia

Responding to thanks

Ashia – **Good to hear that the event went so well.** Very happy to help in Riyadh. Send me the details when you have them.

Donna

Notes

Just a quick note to say many thanks …

Note the use of *just* to indicate the start of a short message:
Just to say I have received your message.
Just to remind you that I'll be away next week.

We really appreciate everything you have done.

To *appreciate* is to *value*. The use of *really* makes the meaning even stronger.

Many congratulations on your promotion.

The use of *many* at the beginning of the sentence adds a note of friendliness. Note also:
Many thanks for all your help.
Many apologies for the delay in sending this.

… stay in touch.

Use this when you would like to keep in contact. You can also say: *Keep in touch.*
I hope we don't lose touch.

This is to let you know that I will be leaving EFPC …

This is to let you know that … is a useful way to announce the reason for sending an email. Note also:
Just to let you know that …

Please come and visit me …

Other friendly invitations to visit:
Please come and see me when you are in Bristol.
You are always welcome here.
You must come and see us soon.

I was very sorry to hear that you are leaving the company.

You could also write:
I was very sad to hear about it.
We will all miss you.
It won't be the same without you.

It has been a pleasure working with you …

You could also say:
I have really enjoyed working with you.
It's been great working with you. (more informal)

… I wish you every success in the future.

Sending good wishes:
Good luck in the future.
Good luck with your new job.
Enjoy your retirement.

Thanks for all your help …

More formal:
Thank you very much for everything.
I am very grateful for all you have done.
I really appreciated your help.

It would be great to see you there.

Some alternative phrases:
I'd be very pleased if you could come.
I'd be delighted if you could make it.
I'd be very glad if you could help.

Good to hear that the event went so well.

You can also write:
It was good to hear …
Note how words can be left out in informal emails to people we know. Other examples:
Very happy to help = <u>I am</u> very happy to help
Sorry to hear about it = <u>I was</u> sorry to hear about it.
Look forward to hearing from you = <u>I</u> look forward to hearing from you

British/American differences

British	American
I was sorry to hear that you are leaving.	I am sorry to hear that you are leaving. Note: American English often uses the present tense for this kind of expression.
Stay in touch.	Keep in touch. (also used in British English)
Many congratulations. In written English, *Many* is added here for emphasis.	Congratulations. *Many* is not used in this way in American English.
I will be leaving EPFC.	I am leaving EPFC.
… my mobile number.	… my cell (phone) number.
I wish you every success for the future. (*every success* is not used in American English)	Best of luck in the future. (also used in British English) (*I wish you …* is not often used in American English)

71

Messages 2

Good news

Heli

I'm pleased to tell you that **I've just received the results** of the latest customer satisfaction survey and the results are very good. **I thought you'd like to know immediately.** I heard that you're coming into the office next week. Hope to see you then.

Macy

Replying to good news

Well done, Macy. You've done a great job! I'll be in the office on Thursday so we can go through the results together.

Heli

Bad news

Dear Olga

I'm sorry to tell you that George will be on sick leave for two weeks. As you know, he has not been very well for some time. I'll be looking after his work while he is away so if you need anything, please contact me.

Regards

Tim

Replying to bad news

Dear George

I was really sorry to hear you're not well. I know you'll be worried about your work, but I'm sure that Tim can handle things! Take care and make sure you get plenty of rest.

Get well soon.

Olga

A reminder

Dear Sarah

Have you remembered that Mona is retiring in June?

We'd like to organise a leaving party for her. **I hope you can make it. I'm sure she'd want you to be there.** By the way, do you think she would like some golf equipment as a retirement present?

Regards

Duncan

Replying to a reminder

Duncan – **Thank you for reminding me** about Mona's retirement. I'm sure she would really appreciate some new golf clubs – but I recommend that you ask her what she would like before you buy them! **Just to check** – is the retirement party going to be in June? **If so, I'd love to come.** I'll be on holiday from June 30.

Best wishes

Sarah

Notes

I'm pleased to tell you …

Other ways to introduce good news:
Good news! I've just received the results …
I'm happy to tell you the results.
You'll be pleased to know that the results are very good.

… I've just received the results …

More phrases for announcing news:
I've just heard that …
John has just told me that …
I heard from John that …
Did you know that …

I thought you'd like to know immediately.

It is very common to use I thought or I knew to announce news:
I thought you'd be interested to hear …
I thought you might not know that …
I knew you wanted to know the results.

Well done, Macy.

An alternative to Congratulations!
Using the name (Well done, Macy) personalises the congratulations.

I'm sorry to tell you that George will be on sick leave for two weeks.

If you want to say more:
He has been unwell for some time.
He has just had an operation.
He has broken his leg.

I was really sorry to hear you're not well.

Other expressions of sympathy:
I was sorry to hear that you have been ill.
I was very sorry to hear about the accident.
I was shocked to hear about it.

Get well soon.

An alternative: Hope you feel better soon.
You may also see this formal alternative:
We wish you a speedy recovery.

Have you remembered that Mona is retiring in June?

Have you remembered that … and Just to remind you are polite ways of reminding someone. Compare with:
Have you forgotten that …

I hope you can make it.

To make it (informal) means to come/attend.
I hope you can make it to the meeting.
I hope you can make it on Tuesday.

I'm sure she'd want you to be there.

Use I'm sure when you believe something is true.
I'm sure I told you about it.
I'm sure he agreed to come.
I'm not sure indicates uncertainty:
I'm not sure if I told you.
I'm not sure who is coming.

Thank you for reminding me …

Note how we use Thank you for +ing:
Thank you for helping me.
Thank you for sending the report.

Just to check …

Other phrases to check meaning:
Just checking –
Can I just check …
More formal ways to ask for clarification:
Can you explain what you meant by …
I'm sorry, but could you please clarify …

If so, I'd love to come.

If so means If this is true or If this is the case.

British/American differences

British	American
Well done! (Not used in American English.)	Good job!
I'll be looking after his work …	I'll be taking care of his work … (Also used in British English, though less frequently.)
A leaving party	A farewell party
I'll be on holiday from June 30. (pronounced June the thirtieth)	I'll be on vacation starting June 30. (pronounced June thirtieth)
He has just had an operation./He has broken his leg.	He just had an operation./He broke his leg.
I was really sorry to hear …	I'm/I am really sorry to hear …
Equipment Booking Form	Equipment Reservation Form

Practice

1 Make these statements more 'friendly'. Refer to the messages in the chapter and the phrases below

EXAMPLE: Please come and visit us. ....

a Have a rest!
   Make sure ....

b Thank you.
   Many ....

c Sonja has broken her arm.
   I'm sorry to ....

d John is retiring next month.
   Just to let ....

e I will come to the party.
   I'd ....

f I hope you can attend the meeting.
   I hope you can ....

g He wants some sports equipment for his leaving present.
   I'm sure he'd ....

h Contact me.
   Please get in ....

2 Complete the sentences with a form of the word in brackets.

EXAMPLE: I have really enjoyed .... working with you.   (enjoyment)

a Are you looking forward to your ....   (retire)

b I'm organising a .... for Mona.   (collect)

c We really.................... all the help you have given us.   (appreciation)

d Just to let you know about Laura's ....   (promote)

e We were all .... when we heard the news.   (shock)

f Could you .... exactly what is happening?   (clarification)

g I have an important .... to make!   (announce)

h Many .... Very well done!   (congratulate)

i I was sorry to hear about your .... leg.   (break)

j I hope you are feeling better after the ....   (operate)

3 Put the sentences below in the correct order.

a   to hearing from you.
b   for helping to organise the office party.
c   Many thanks
d   your help again.
e   It was a great success!
f   Could you call me

g   We are planning to arrange
h   to discuss this.
i   All the best
j   Looking forward
k   and we would really appreciate
l   another event in December

Hi Ian
   c Many thanks ....
....
....
....
....
....
....
....

Conchita

4 Match the two parts of the sentences.

1   I was very sorry to
2   Just to remind you
3   We are planning to organise
4   I'm sure that Rosa
5   She had to leave the company
6   I have decided to
7   Good to
8   I'd be delighted if
9   It has been a

a   would like to come to the party.
b   move back to Dubai.
c   hear that everything went well.
d   that Frieda is retiring next week.
e   hear that you haven't been well.
f   for personal reasons.
g   a leaving party for her.
h   pleasure working with you.
i   you could visit us in the summer.

5 Complete the puzzle below and find the keyword.

				p	l	e	a	s	e	
1				p	l	e	a	s	e	
2		w								
3								r		
4						s				
5				s						s
6	t									
7	a									
8				e					g	

1 .Please......... keep in touch!

2 You are very . . . . to come and stay with us.

3 Have you . . . . that it is Julie's birthday tomorrow?

4 Many . . . . for all your help!

5 We wish you every . . . . in the future.

6 I . . . . you'd like to hear the news immediately.

7 We really . . . . all your help.

8 I was sorry to hear that you are . . . . the company.

KEYWORD = P . . . .

6 Complete the sentences with a preposition.

EXAMPLE: Congratulations .on . . . . your promotion.

a I was sorry to hear . . . . your accident.

b We are very grateful . . . . all your help.

c I hope you are feeling better. Get plenty . . . . rest.

d I going to be . . . . holiday next week.

e I'm afraid Kate is . . . . sick leave.

f Who looks . . . . Kate's work when she is away?

g I'll be back . . . . Friday? See you then.

h Thank you . . . . reminding me.

Glossary

1 The Basics

Beginnings and endings	Your language
Hi Kim	....
How are you?	....
I'm finalising the details of the Leadership Course.	....
Best regards	....
No changes needed. (No changes are needed).	....
Dear Ms Novotna – Yours sincerely	....
I would like to invite you to visit us.	....
I look forward to meeting you again.	....
Dear Sir/Madam – Yours faithfully	....
This is to confirm that your current policy covers you.	....

Basic layout

It was good to meet you at the seminar in Paris.	....
I would like to arrange a meeting with you.	....
We have many new products that will interest you.	....
Could you let me know if you are available on June 5th or 6th?	....
I look forward to hearing from you soon.	....
Please note that our Korean agent will be visiting the company next Friday 21 June.	....
Please confirm that you can attend.	....
Dear all,	....
I've attached a copy of the menu for the annual dinner.	....
Laurent, please can you make the arrangements for the music?	....

2 Making Contact

Messages 1   Your language

I have seen your advertisement on your web   . . . .
page.   . . . .

I would like to apply for the post.   . . . .

I am currently working as a Marketing Assistant. . . . .

I work for a publishing company in London.   . . . .

Thank you for your email.   . . . .

I am pleased to attach our online application   . . . .
form.   . . . .

I look forward to your reply.   . . . .

I enclose my CV as requested.   . . . .

Please let me know if you have any queries.   . . . .

I apologise for not sending this earlier.   . . . .

Please call me on my mobile.   . . . .

Messages 2

We are writing to invite you to a conference.   . . . .

Please take a look at our website.   . . . .

I am sending the schedule for the   . . . .
forthcoming conference.   . . . .

We would like to attend the conference.   . . . .

We have reserved a stand for you.   . . . .

Could you please send us a summary of your   . . . .
company by the end of the week?   . . . .

We are an established company in the UK.   . . . .

We provide training for the manufacturing   . . . .
and service industries.   . . . .

We are happy to provide on-site training.   . . . .

We can provide training at venues in the UK.   . . . .

3 Arrangements

Arranging a visit

We would be very pleased if you could visit   . . . .
our company.   . . . .

Please let us know your availability.   . . . .

Thank you for the invitation to visit your company. . . . .

I look forward to your confirmation. ....

Just to confirm your visit to us next Friday. ....

See you Friday. ....

I am attaching a map with directions to our
   facility. ....
....

Follow the road around to the main reception. ....

Do you know when you are planning to arrive
   yet? ....
....

Travel arrangements

I've put together the following itinerary. ....

We need to finalise it today. ....

Departure is from Milan at 11:05 on flight BA68. ....

You will have an overnight stay at the Hilton Hotel
   in Salford. ....
....

Your pick-up by company car will be at 8:00. ....

I'm booking Don's flights today for the Berlin
   meeting. ....
....

The Lufthansa flight leaves London at 7:30. ....

Shall I reserve you a seat on the same flights? ....

I am writing to confirm the reservation. ....

Could you check out the following for me
   please? ....
....

Has the airline reserved an aisle seat for me? ....

Taking and forwarding messages

I'm sorry I wasn't free to speak. ....

I tried to call you back this afternoon. ....

The number was engaged. ....

Jane Baxter has been delayed in Shanghai. ....

Can you give her apologies, please? ....

There are still some details to sort out. ....

Can he call her tonight, please? ....

I've just received the draft itinerary for Sweden
   from Helen. ....
....

Have a look at it. ....

Thanks for this, Stefan. ....

Let's say 10 a.m. in my office. . . . .

I shall be away from the office until 22 July. . . . .

4 Meetings

Setting up a meeting (1)

We need to set up a meeting. . . . .

How about next week sometime? . . . .

What about Tuesday at 1 p.m. in the canteen? . . . .

We could have a working lunch. . . . .

I would be very pleased to visit you next Tuesday. . . . .

3 p.m. would be fine with me. . . . .

I look forward to seeing you again next week. . . . .

Can you confirm the meeting on 21st in Bonn? . . . .

We need to finalise arrangements today. . . . .

I want to meet urgently. . . . .

The purpose of the meeting is to brief you on the . . . .

   meeting. . . . .

Please clear your diaries. . . . .

Setting up a meeting (2)

Please let me know in advance if you are unable . . . .

   to attend. . . . .

Agenda/Venue/Participants/Apologies . . . .

I've attached the minutes of the last meeting. . . . .

AOB/Date of next meeting . . . .

Please note the change to item 2 on the agenda. . . . .

I've moved the International Strategies paper to . . . .

   next week. . . . .

We'll need to circulate the agenda prior to the . . . .

   meeting. . . . .

Our computer system is down. . . . .

Is it possible to put this on the agenda for . . . .

   Monday's meeting? . . . .

I'd like to run through the final arrangements. . . . .

We need to ensure that everything runs smoothly. . . . .

Meeting follow-up

Review of last quarter's performance	. . . .
All teams to provide weekly report.	. . . .
Schedule interviews with the Press.	. . . .
AOB = any other business	. . . .
I've just looked at the minutes.	. . . .
We'll need to rearrange a date.	. . . .
I suggest the 2nd June.	. . . .
Can you please send out an amendment to everyone?	. . . .
Re. the new brochures …	. . . .
By the way, I was interested to see our new sales target.	. . . .
Thanks for your comments on our performance.	. . . .
I've passed on your congratulations to the team.	. . . .
Thank you for all your support.	. . . .

5 Enquiries

Messages 1

Please send me a current price list.	. . . .
Could you include some samples?	. . . .
Thank you for your interest in our products.	. . . .
Your email was forwarded to me.	. . . .
We believe in buying from Fairtrade organisations.	. . . .
You will find further information on our website.	. . . .
I will send you a copy of our new catalogue.	. . . .
Many thanks for your prompt response.	. . . .
We are very interested in ordering from you.	. . . .
Would May 24th be a suitable time to visit you?	. . . .
I enclose a copy of our latest company brochure.	. . . .

Message 2

What would you advise us to do?	. . . .
Are there any suppliers that you recommend?	. . . .
It's best not to start the machine again until the engineer arrives.	. . . .

Your language

Have you considered contacting Gudul? . . . .

You could contact Universal Tools. . . . .

I would be grateful if you could send me further . . . .
information. . . . .

Thank you for your enquiry. . . . .

I'm afraid we do not run any general courses. . . . .

I have forwarded your enquiry to Filton College. . . . .

With reference to your enquiry. . . . .

You can see further details of our school by . . . .
going to our website. . . . .

6 Orders, dealing with problems
Orders

We have recently ordered some new office . . . .
furniture. . . . .

Could you please quote for removal of existing . . . .
furniture. . . . .

We would like to place an order with you. . . . .

Your terms and conditions state a delivery time . . . .
of four weeks. . . . .

Would it be possible to dispatch the items within . . . .
two weeks? . . . .

If there is an additional charge, please let us . . . .
know. . . . .

I can confirm that all the items you ordered are . . . .
in stock. . . . .

We'd like a repeat order. . . . .

Is this your latest catalogue? . . . .

Could you give us a firm delivery date? . . . .

Could you confirm that our usual discount would . . . .
apply? . . . .

Dealing with problems (1)

I'm sorry to say that we may not be able to meet . . . .
the agreed schedule. . . . .

I'm afraid we will fall behind schedule. ....

Your language

I was very surprised to receive your message. ....

You assured us that this schedule was
  guaranteed. ....

On Friday 13th March we took delivery of a
  consignment of CD cases. ....

On unpacking the boxes, we found that many of
  the cases were damaged. ....

This is extremely inconvenient for us. ....

We urgently need replacements. ....

I am very sorry to hear that you had problems
  with our delivery. ....

We have sent a replacement by courier. ....

Our regular packer was on holiday. ....

Our service was below our usual standard. ....

Dealing with problems (2)

We are very unhappy with the level of service
  you have given us this year. ....

We always have to wait for spare parts. ....

We have had to shut down production on three
  occasions. ....

I was very sorry to hear about the problems you
  have experienced. ....

We should meet as soon as I hear the outcome. ....

I expect to receive his report by the end of this
  week. ....

We have still not received this order. ....

We apologise for any misunderstanding. ....

We do try to keep our website up-to-date. ....

I regret that we cannot accept the return as
  faulty goods. ....

As a goodwill gesture, we will issue a credit note. ....

I trust this meets with your approval. ....

7 Short reports

Providing information   Your language

Could you send me a short report? . . . .

We hold weekly Board meetings. . . . .

The purpose of the visit was to take part in the . . . .
  Exhibition. . . . .

2 000 enquiries were received. . . . .

We need to follow up customer enquiries . . . .
  immediately. . . . .

We recommend that the new agents should visit . . . .
  the UK. . . . .

Just one thing missing – can you send me the . . . .
  cost analysis? . . . .

Exhibition stand . . . .

Expenses/Expenditure/Anticipated Revenue . . . .

Focus on Facts and Figures

This year we had over 25 000 visitors. . . . .

A third of the visitors were children under sixteen. . . . .

Approximately 90 per cent of the visitors said . . . .
  they found the Centre informative. . . . .

Most people were happy to pay the entrance . . . .
  fee of $3.50. . . . .

Sales went up by 30 per cent. . . . .

There was a sharp rise of 40 per cent. . . . .

Sales dropped slightly by 2 per cent. . . . .

Compared with last quarter, sales are higher. . . . .

Last year's fall in productivity was a direct . . . .
  result of low morale. . . . .

These pay cuts were responsible for the . . . .
  increase in sick leave. . . . .

8 Personal messages

Messages 1

Just a quick note to say many thanks. . . . .

We really appreciate everything you have done. . . . .

Many congratulations on your promotion. . . . .

Your language

Stay in touch. ....

This is to let you know that I will be leaving EFPC. ....

Please come and visit me. ....

I was very sorry to hear that you are leaving
   the company. ....
   ....

It has been a pleasure working with you. ....

I wish you every success in the future. ....

Thanks for all your help. ....

It would be great to see you there. ....

Good to hear that the event went so well. ....

Messages 2

I'm pleased to tell you that I've just received
   the results. ....
   ....

I thought you'd like to know immediately. ....

Well done, Macy. ....

I'm sorry to tell you that George will be on sick
   leave for two weeks. ....
   ....

I was really sorry to hear that you're not well. ....

Get well soon. ....

Have you remembered that Mona is retiring
   in June? ....
   ....

We'd like to organise a collection for her. ....

I hope you can make it. ....

I'm sure she'd want you to be there. ....

Thank you for reminding me. ....

Just to check – is the party in June? ....

If so, I'd love to come. ....

Answers

1 The Basics

1 a – i, b – i, c – ii, d – i, e – ii

2 a i b ii c i d ii e ii f i

3 a to b at c to d for e on, at f on g at h for

4 a check b receiving c meeting d visiting e know f go
g writing h confirm

5 1 e 2 f 3 b 4 c 5 h 6 g 7 d 8 a

6 **An informal message**
1 c 2 d 3 a 4 g 5 f 6 b 7 h 8 e

A formal memo
1 b 2 d 3 a 4 c 5 h 6 g 7 f 8 e

7 **Memorandum**

To:	All Staff
From:	(your name) Human Resources Manager
Date:	(today's date)
Subject:	Health and Safety Conference

I would like to invite you all to attend a conference on July 22, at 9 a.m.
in the Board Room. There will be a buffet lunch at midday.
Please confirm that you can attend.
If you have any queries please do not hesitate to contact me on extension 345.

2 Making Contact

1 a as b for c at d as e by f on g at h in

2 1 iii 2 v 3 ii 4 i 5 vi 6 iv

3 a on-site b range c producer d service e summary f questionnaire

4 1 d 2 g 3 a 4 e 5 b 6 c 7 f

5 Dear Colleague
2 We are writing to inform you
5 that we are organising a conference in New York
7 at the end of the month.
6 We would like to invite
8 your organisation to attend.
1 Please take a look at our website at www.conzfi.co.kr
4 where you will find full details of the conference.
3 Please do not hesitate to contact us
9 if you require any further information.
Yours sincerely
Jeongmi Seo

6   1 b   2 c   3 d   4 a

7   The Customer is always right
John Smith
Laptop, projector, video
4th October
Conference Room B

3 Arrangements

1   a confirm   single   22nd July
b pleased   next week   stay
c office   contact   queries
d invitation   August   attend

2   1 e   2 a   3 i   4 b   5 c   6 d   7 f   8 g   9 h

3   1 b   2 a   3 f   4 c   5 d   6 e

4   a along; on   b in; at   c at; at   d from/to/for   e for   f on; to

5   a correct   b not necessary   c correct   d not necessary   e incorrect – for
f correct   g incorrect – away   h incorrect – at

6   Marketing
To attend Agents Workshop
17th June 11:45
Air France
Credit card

4 Meetings

1   a availability   b manage   c suit   d available   e suits

2   1 We'll need to
2 Thank you for
3 Can you pass on
4 Can you confirm
5 Please let me know
6 I would be very pleased
7 What about

3   1 iii   2 v   3 vi   4 viii   5 vii   6 ii   7 i   8 iv

4

1 agenda
2 available
3 participants
4 diary
5 reschedule
6 amendments
7 brief
8 minutes
9 apologies
10 item
11 circulate
12 summary

KEYWORD = availability

```
        ¹A G E N D A
                A V A I L A B L E
    ³P A R T I C I P A N T S
                ⁴D I A R Y
    ⁵R E S C H E D U L E
                    ⁶A M E N D M E N T S
                    ⁷B R I E F
              ⁸M I N U T E S
          ⁹A P O L O G I E S
                    ¹⁰I T E M
    ¹¹C I R C U L A T E
          ¹²S U M M A R Y
```

5 Example answer

To all Marketing Staff

There will be a meeting on Tuesday 14th in the Conference Room from 14:00 to 16:00 to discuss the new brochure. Please let me know in advance if you are unable to attend.

Looking forward to seeing you all next week.

Pierre

6 a in; at b at; on c for; on; by d with; at; at e in f on; in

5 Enquiries

1 a in b in c for d to e for f in g With; to

2 a to hear b to start c to be d to arrive e solving f buying g using
h getting i going

3 a Some information is in the post.
b The report is attached.
c What is your advice?
d Our company strongly recommends EDR.
e What about closing down the system first?
f I'm sorry but we do not arrange delivery.

4 a ii b ii c ii d i e ii f ii g i

5 1 e 2 c 3 f 4 h 5 a 6 b 7 i 8 d 9 g

6 Enquiry 1
1 b 2 d 3 a 4 e 5 f 6 c 7 h 8 g
Enquiry 2
1 d 2 b 3 e 4 c 5 a 6 g 7 f

7 a contacting b recommendation c advice d enquiry
e reliable f logging g attached h forwarded

6 Orders, dealing with problems

1 a order b forward c assured d accept e dispatched f meet

2 a to b on c for d with e by f for g on h for i with

3 1 e 2 f 3 h 4 g 5 a 6 b 7 d 8 i 9 c

4 a have experienced b to discuss c to receive d have sent
    e return, will refund f apologise

5 a dissatisfied b dispatch c additional d definite e a discount
    f concerned g promise h a refund i meet

6

> Dear Ms Duval
>
> Thank you for your letter.
>
> I was very sorry to hear that you had problems with our consignment of printers.
>
> We have sent a replacement order to you today by courier. The same courier will take away the damaged printers, at no extra cost.
>
> I trust this meets with your approval.
>
> Please accept our apologies.
>
> Yours sincerely
> *(Sign your name)*
> *(Print your name)*

7 Short Reports

1 A 2 This report shows the breakdown of sales during the last year.
    B 1 Sales worldwide rose by 18 per cent in the last quarter.
        3 Europe still has the largest share of the market.
        6 Sales in the Far East fell by 3 per cent.
    C 4 We need to increase our advertising in the Far East.
        7 We must appoint new agents in the Far East.
    D 5 Overall, business was very good last year and we expect this success to continue.

2 a steady b sharp c due to d in e increase f competitive
    g investing h Overall i higher

3 1 purpose
    2 a visitors c placed
    3 a recommendation b recommend due
    4 due

4

```
a   d   e   c   l   i   n   e
z   p   b   a   e   l   s   m
o   s   i   b   e   a   m   o
r   q   n   d   e   f   p   b
i   n   c   r   e   a   s   e
s   o   c   o   e   l   l   m
e   e   d   p   c   l   b   s
d   i   m   p   r   o   v   e
```

5

A	rose	a sharp decline	improvement	(Graph 2)
B	the least	very low	resulted in	(Graph 3)
C	successful	due to	drop	(Graph 1)

8 Personal messages

1
a Make sure you get plenty of rest.
b Many thanks
c I'm sorry to hear that Sonja has broken her arm.
d Just to let you know that John is retiring next month.
e I'd love to come to the party.
f I hope you can make it to the meeting.
g I'm sure he'd really appreciate/like some sports equipment for his leaving present.
h Please get in touch (with me).

2 a retirement b collection c appreciate d promotion e shocked f clarify
g announcement h congratulations i broken f operation

3 Hi Ian
c Many thanks
b for helping to organise the party
e It was a great success!
g We are planning to arrange
l another event in December
k and we would really appreciate
d your help again.
f Could you call me
h to discuss this.

  j Looking forward
  a to hearing from you.
  i All the best
Conchita

4   1 e 2 d 3 g 4 a 5 f 6 b 7 c 8 i 9 h

5   1 please
     2 welcome
     3 remembered
     4 thanks
     5 success
     6 thought
     7 appreciate
     8 leaving
     KEYWORD = pleasure

6   a about b for c of d on e on f after g on h for

Punctuation

Emails are often written very quickly, and rules of punctuation are not always followed. However, correct use of punctuation makes the message clearer. Some examples:

An apostrophe (contraction)
I'll send you the report as soon as possible.
(I'll = I will)

An apostrophe (possessive)
John's schedule.

Brackets
Tel: **(**01423**)** 187900

A colon
We will need the following**:**
50 chairs
5 desks
1 digital projector

A comma
The new director**,** Fred Cuplet**,** will be in the office tomorrow.

A dash
Saleh **–** can you call me tomorrow.

A dot
The web address is efpc**.**co**.**uk/info

An exclamation mark
Well done everyone**!**

A full stop
I'll try and call you tomorrow at 3 p**.**m**.**

A hyphen
I'd prefer to have a right**-**hand drive car.

Quotation marks
Mayumi said she was **"**pleased**"** with the results.

A question mark
Have we forgotten anything**?**

A semi-colon
Business is going well**;** we have increased sales by 20 per cent.

A slash
The web address is efpc.co.uk**/**info

Dates and times

Dates

There are several ways to write the date:
I have been working as a Marketing Manager since 16 July 2002.
The contract was signed on March 30 2001.
Production of the CP4 model started on 10.07.01.
Toni will retire on 23rd November 2002.
See you at 2 p.m. on Thursday 3 Sept.

When you write the date, you can leave out the letters (*-st, -nd, -rd, -th*) that follow the number, but you always say *first, second, third, fourth etc.* whether you write it or not:
3 July 2001 – the third of July, two thousand and one, or July the third, two thousand and one
31st December – the thirty-first of December

You can write the date completely in figures *10.07.03*, but to make sure there is no misunderstanding it is better to write it in full *10th July 2003* or *July 10th 2003*

Common Expressions of Time

For

We have been exporting to Brazil for three years.
I have been trying to contact you for two days.
(*For* refers to a period of time, showing how long something has lasted.*)*

Since

I have been waiting since the beginning of August for a reply.
We've been supplying these materials since 2002.
(*Since* gives the starting point of actions continuing up to the present.*)*

Ago

I left a message three days ago.
I visited Hamburg many years ago.
(*Ago* shows when a past action started but not by giving actual dates.*)*

Last

I enjoyed meeting you last week.
The conference last year was a great success.

Next

I look forward to seeing you next Monday.
The goods will be ready for delivery next week.

Until

I will be at the office until 8 p.m. tonight.
I'm going to stay with the company until September.

Prepositions of Time

In

Can you confirm a delivery date in July?
I left the company in 2003.
In (the) summer, sales went up substantially.
John Smith is retiring in 2007.

At

Are you available at 2 o'clock tomorrow?
The company will be closed at Christmas.
The office is open at the weekend.

On

I look forward to meeting you on Tuesday.
We will deliver the goods on Friday 17 May.

By

The cases should arrive by Monday.
The minutes will be ready by Tuesday lunchtime.
(By refers to a deadline)

From

There will be a meeting in the conference room from 2 to 5 p.m.
I was in Berlin from 4th to 8th July.

British/American differences

British	American
July the third, two thousand and one	*July third, two thousand one*
10/07/03 (10th July 2003)	*10/7/03 (October 7th 2003)* **NOTE:** American English style is month/day/year
The company will be closed at Christmas.	*The company will be closed on Christmas.* **NOTE:** In the US only December 25th is a holiday so *on* is used. If the period of closing is longer, one can say *'closed for the holidays'.*
The office is open at the weekend.	*The office is open on the weekend.*

Abbreviations

Some common abbreviations used in emails.

a.m.	before midday *(ante meridiem)*, e.g. 9:00 a.m.
approx.	approximately
ASAP	as soon as possible
Attn	For the attention of
cc	copy to
co.	company
CV	curriculum vitae
dept.	department
e.g.	for example *(exemplii gratia)*
ETA	estimated time of arrival
etc.	et cetera
FAO	For the attention of (FAO is not used in American English)
FYI	For your information
govt.	government
i.e.	that is *(id est)*
Inc.	Incorporated
Ltd	Limited
N.B.	Please note *(Nota bene)*
pcs	pieces
p.m.	after midday *(post meridiem)*
pp*	on behalf of *(per pro)*
PS	Postscript
qty	quantity
re.	regarding
ref.	reference
RSVP	Please reply *(Répondez s'il vous plait)*
tba	to be advised/to be agreed
tbc	to be confirmed

* pp is not used in American English. When you sign a document on behalf of another person, you can write the person's name followed by your initials.